David J

Never fear to stand as a
patriot !

Table of Contents

Publisher's Note

The opinions expressed in this book are the opinions of the authors, and tend to be very conservative and Judeo-Christian in nature. Those of a liberal mindset ... enter at your own risk.

This will be your only warning.

Foreword

America provides the most freedom and is the most prosperous nation in the world, but we are quickly sliding away from the principles and values that have produced and sustained this wonderful nation.

Our nation began, as intended by our founding fathers, with a culture based on Judeo-Christian values. Yet we see anti-Semitism and attacks on people and businesses who seek to live by those values. Many of our public schools prohibit the practice of Christianity while teaching the practice of Islam. Accurate history is rare, and rarely focuses on the people and activities that truly impacted our nation or our world. We are hyper focused on foreign, minority, and politically correct issues in schools, businesses, and government.

This must change.

It is our hope and intent that this book will raise some of the key issues that real patriots must, first, be aware of, and, second, take action to re-establish our nation's foundation.

If not you, then, who? If not now, then, when?

ISBN 978-1-61808-191-9
Printed in the United States of America

The photography in this book is owned by Rick Vuyst and used with his permission.
Cover design created by Ron Bell of AdVision Design Group (www.advisiondesigngroup.com)
Declaration of Independence photo ©iStockphoto.com/ Stefan Klein

White Feather Press

Reaffirming Faith in God, Family, and Country!

FRONTLINES

OF

FREEDOM

Field Manual by
Vets for Patriots
How to Save America

written by

AMERICAN MILITARY
VETERANS

Dedication

This book is dedicated to:

Those who have served in our nation's military – the sword assaulting our enemies

The families—and extended families—of those who have served in our military

The police who have served our nation—the shield protecting our nation.

The American patriots who support our military and first responders

But, primarily, this book is dedicated to the children in America. This nation must return to its Godly, caring, serving culture—or they will not inherit a free and prosperous nation.

INTRODUCTION

THIS BOOK IS WRITTEN BY US military veterans. You may count on the fact that these authors love our nation—because each one has elected to serve. Not all were called to actually serve in combat, but all were ready to serve there, if our country needed them.

It's generally understood that, if you get something for nothing, then you don't value it as much as something that you had to pay to get. Our nation's veterans have paid—by placing their lives at the disposal of our nation—for our freedoms. We value this wonderful nation that offers so much to its citizens and has done so much good in the world—this is not to suggest in any way that our nation is perfect or always right. It is to say that we have very little competition as the greatest provider of peace and prosperity in the world.

We see so many people hyper-concerned about their rights to get free things from the government and the ability to do or say whatever they wish with no consequences. These same people seem to have no vision of an obligation to serve their community or nation.

It's not okay to support our nation's one and only real ally, Israel; instead, we are pressured to support the Muslim terrorists who attack Israeli schools, hospitals and civilians. We're not allowed to discuss the brutality and absence of rights that women and Christians are subject to in all Muslim nations.

We can't discuss that there are only two genders and that while men and women are equal, they are still very different—and it's more than just the plumbing. It is demanded that women be admitted to the Army infantry and Navy SEALs, yet there is no pressure for them to play in the NFL or NHL—or PGA.

As you read through the chapters, we hope you will be challenged to get involved in redirecting our nation back to our Godly values. No one can get involved in everything, but we can all do something and recruit others to the cause. It's our nation. We are losing it to the Politically Correct crowd. We must take it back for our children and their children.

SPECIAL RECOGNITION

The Medal of Honor Foundation's Character Development Program truly impacts our nation's youth with the insights and values they need.

The Wounded Warrior Project supports our brave troops who have been injured while serving our nation; we must help these veterans return to society as productive members.

We have no relationship with either of these two organizations, but we consider them great role models for returning our nation to our proper values.

We encourage you to support these great non-profit organizations.

stewardship [stoo-erd-ship]
-noun-
1: the office, duties, and obli-
gations of a steward
2: the conducting, supervis-
ing, or managing of something
especially: the careful and
responsible management of
something entrusted to one's
care

– Merriam Webster

CHAPTER 1

OUR NATION NEEDS US TO BE GOOD STEWARDS

BY DENNY GILLEM

Americans have inherited the most free and prosperous nation on earth.

To keep it free and prosperous we must be good stewards.

I**F YOU INHERIT A CAR, YOU DO MORE** than keep it full of gas and drive it when you wish. You must also change the oil, get it tuned, keep the air in the tires, and replace worn parts or it will soon be a piece of junk on the side of the road.

If you inherit a house, you do more than live in it. It must be kept clean and repaired and the grass cut—or it will soon be a mold-filled place where only rats can live.

We are quickly losing the values that made our nation great and have sustained us for generations. Our education system teaches made-up history; our students are taught "what" to think, not "how" to think. Most citizens cannot name many of their elected officials and have never been in contact with any of them—and have no idea how they perform their duties; this is why the swamps in Washington DC and many state capitals thrive— officials are rarely held accountable.

It is time for Americans to become good stewards of America!

Good Americans come in all political flavors. But open, honest discussion of issues—which can produce understanding and reasonable compromise, has too often been replaced with name-calling, hatred, close mindedness, and, sometimes, violence. This must stop.

Our nation is so focused on being politically correct that many have abandoned both moral values and common sense. It's more important to have a diverse team than to be effective in what you do. We can't speak truth if it might offend someone. One can't give a business or product a name that might be offensive to anyone. It may not be long before every NFL team will be forced to have one short, weak woman for every tall, strong man. This is nonsense.

American Military Veterans

In our new culture it's fine to belittle Christians and Jews in any way, but it's totally inappropriate to point out that all of the Muslim nations in the world are dictatorships and that killing others is a part of many (not all) Muslims' theology. Similarly, it's expected to condemn Israel for every action, yet the terrorists that target Israeli civilians, schools, and hospitals while teaching their children to hate and kill all Jews are just fine.

There is a lack of respect for authority.

This is especially noted in the anti-police attitude in many communities. As our military is our sword to attack foreign enemies, our police are the shield to protect our citizens. They put their lives on the line every day to protect people—some of whom don't even like them. Some days they are required to make life-or-death decisions in a micro-second, and then they are sometimes judged by people who are biased against them. If we want to keep good police officers, we must take care of them and show them the respect they deserve.

Our education system is broken. Our students don't learn accurate American history or how our government works. They don't know the difference between capitalism and socialism. Many students don't know why we celebrate the 4th of July. Federal control of education—which is contrary to our Constitution—keeps communities that need plumbers from teaching plumbing in school, yet mandates algebra for all.

Dare we say that children raised in single-parent homes are much more likely to fail in school, join gangs, be jailed, and become a drain on society?

> *A primary purpose of a military is to*
> *kill people and break things.*

If our military is really good at this, then bad guys won't want to mess with us. That's deterrence. When we do need them to confront and attack an enemy, the military will do so with a minimum loss of life for our troops. When considering possible changes within the military structure, shouldn't combat readiness be given priority? Yet, the politically correct crowd wants us to use government funds for gender-change operations and deal with the non-deployable person while he/she recovers. We now have women in close combat (infantry, armor, special ops) units. There is a difference between males and females—and it's more than the plumbing. Why are there no women playing in the NFL or NHL? Note that, in the professional golf world, there is a PGA and an LPGA. Contact sports involve non-lethal combat; but women can be in the infantry and engage hand-to-hand with the enemy—in lethal combat, no less! In combat, consider also sexual tension. If a male and a female like each other, how does that work on a long combat operation? Yes, there will be consequences. Or, if I like one of the ladies in my Ranger unit—and another guy does too, we're now competitors, no longer team-mates, we're competitors, and we are going into combat. Really?

Leaders are to look out for their troops and protect them.

Our military leaders have for years allowed some of their combat troops to be charged with murder for killing the enemy in combat. What kind of leaders can do that?

In such circumstances, real leaders would object or resign if forced to prosecute, rather than fight under obscene rules of engagement. The answer is that too many leaders seemingly wish to be seen as politically correct.

There's more—lots more. The goal of the book, Frontlines of Freedom, is to identify these areas so that patriotic Americans may become educated, receive some direction, and then take action.

Not everyone can do everything, but we all must do what we can.

It's our nation—and our children will inherit it.

From the Founders

"You will never know how much it has cost my generation to preserve YOUR freedom. I hope you will make a good use of it."

               John Adams

"The price of freedom is eternal vigilance."

           Thomas Jefferson

"What we obtain too cheap, we esteem too lightly: it is dearness only that gives every thing its value. Heaven knows how to put a proper price upon its goods; and it would be strange indeed if so celestial an article as freedom should not be highly rated."

           Thomas Paine

"What country can preserve its liberties if its rulers are not warned from time to time that their people preserve the spirit of resistance? Let them take arms."

           Thomas Jefferson

Lieutenant Colonel Dennis J. Gillem is a 1964 graduate of the United States Military Academy at West Point, and a Vietnam combat veteran. He served two tours in Vietnam as a company grade officer where he received seven US awards for valor. After a distinguished military career he retired and now lives in Michigan with his wife and is an Adjunct Professor of Political Science.

LTC Gillem hosts the nationally syndicated military talk radio show, *Frontlines of Freedom*, which is heard every weekend nation-wide. Go to www.frontlinesoffreedom.com for local station listings and for podcasts.

The Korean War Memorial is dedicated to the sacrifices of the 5.8 million Americans who served in the U.S. armed forces during the 3-year period of the Korean War. Though undeclared by Congress, this war was one of the most hard fought in our history.

A well regulated militia, being
necessary to the security of
a free state, the right of the
people to keep and bear arms,
shall not be infringed.
– Amendment II, US Constitution

CHAPTER 2

THE SECOND AMENDMENT

BY SKIP CORYELL

T HAS BEEN SAID THAT THE Second Amendment is the one right that protects all others ... and that is true. But why is it true? And why do so many people not understand this?

The Second Amendment was vitally important to the Founding Fathers, and that's why they put it right after the freedom of speech, the freedom of the press and the freedom of religion. It stands there as a sentinel, boldly guarding, watching protecting, defying tyranny at every turn without apology. And this frustrates evil to its bitter, black core.

It is undeniable that guns have a special place in the hearts of many freedom-loving Americans. According to the 2018 *Small Arms Survey*, there are over one billion small arms distributed across planet Earth. Of these, 857 million are in civilian hands with the balance being possessed by the world's military and law enforcement agencies.

But what about America? Americans comprise 4 percent of the world's population, but they own 46 percent of the world's guns. American civilians own 393 million guns. Common, ordinary, American citizens own more guns than the combined armed forces of every country on the planet.

SO TELL ME, WHY ARE GUNS SO IMPORTANT TO AMERICANS?

Americans intrinsically know that without the Second Amendment they are defenseless. They are defenseless against violent criminals, against attack from foreign invasion, and, most importantly, from their own government.

I was watching the movie *Lord of the Rings* last night with my family, and was impressed with the opening words of the elf Lady Galadriel when she said:

> *"And some things that should not*
> *have been forgotten were lost.*

History became legend. Legend became myth. And for two and a half thousand years, the ring passed out of all knowledge."

J.R.R. Tolkien,
The Fellowship of the Ring

The overriding purpose for the Second Amendment has nothing to do with hunting or target practice or shooting clays, though all of those activities are beneficial and fun. It's not even about personal protection against criminals. The Founding Fathers believed strongly that if citizens aren't armed, then they are not citizens but mere subjects of a king, serfs under a tyrant, paupers beholden and answerable to a totalitarian regime.

The last line of the Declaration of Independence reads as follows:

"And for the support of this Declaration, with a firm reliance on the protection of Divine Providence, we mutually pledge to each other our Lives, our Fortunes, and our sacred Honor."

Their freedom was more important than money; more valuable than gold or silver, and more precious than their very lives.

Frontlines of Freedom

Today, many Americans take our freedom for granted. We have a lot of it, more than any other country on Earth, thereby appearing to lessen its worth. But we must never let freedom's worth become devalued. We must protect it and defend it at every turn, at every attack, at every attempt to belittle it. Freedom is a currency that, once lost, can only be purchased back by the massive shedding of blood and toil and tears. Our Founders knew that firsthand. They had just fought a long and bloody war against the most powerful military on the planet, and they were determined to never have to do it again.

The *US Constitution* and its accompanying *Bill of Rights* were the blueprint to a lasting liberty, a plan that could be followed for generations to come, provided Americans had the will to continue the venture. Again, I quote Tolkien:

> *"And some things that should not have been forgotten were lost. History became legend. Legend became myth."*

The original meaning of the Second Amendment has been lost by many Americans, especially our younger generation. Why? History has become legend ... legend became myth. The facts are no longer universally believed; indeed, they are disputed at every turn from those who would leach away our freedom and dominate us for the purpose of accruing their own power. Let there be no mistake: there will always be those in this world who would seek to destroy freedom, to dominate their fellow man and to impose their own selfish will on the lives of others. This is the definition of evil.

But the Second Amendment stands in their way, like a sentinel, and like the annoying middle finger of noncompliance.

History has taught us what happens when only governments have guns.

From dictionary.com:

genocide[jen-uh-sahyd]
noun
the deliberate and systematic extermination of a national, racial, political, or cultural group.

The below list of twentieth century genocide is just a sampling of the governments who first disarmed their people before killing them. It was compiled from easy-to-find sources on the internet. Just search on "20th century genocide" to confirm.

The country of Turkey established gun control in 1911, and from 1915-1917, approximately one and a half million Christian Armenians were forcefully collected and exterminated.

The Soviet Union disarmed its subjects in 1929. As a result, between the years 1929-1953, 20 million "political" criminals were rounded up and murdered.

Nazi Germany established gun control in 1938, and from 1939-1945, 13 million Jews and others who were not considered compliant with Hitler or deemed to have impure ancestry were exterminated.

The Chinese government established gun control in the year 1935. In 1949 the communists under Mao Zedong took control and between the years 1948-1952, 20 million political dissidents were systematically executed.

The government of Guatemala established gun control in 1964. Fifteen years later, over a three-

*year period, 100,000 Mayan
Indians were exterminated.*

*Uganda disarmed its public in
1970. Over the next 10 years
300,000 Christians were rounded
up and killed simply for being
Christian.*

*In 1956 Cambodia disarmed its
people, and, from 1975 to 1977,
one million people were imprisoned
and then killed because they were
educated.*

In the 20th Century more than 56 million defenseless people were rounded up and exterminated by governments using gun control. In all
cases they were first legally and forcefully disarmed. They were, in fact and deed, sheep led to
the slaughter.

The Second Amendment says to the tyrant,

*"No, you cannot disarm me. No,
you may not enslave me."*

The other day I was in a mood for a goofy
movie, so I popped in *Monty Python and the
Holy Grail*. In the best comedy, there is always
an element of truth. I was impressed by the Black

Knight, who stood his ground and fought against King Arthur. A summary of the battle ensues below:

The brave and noble King Arthur comes to a bridge, which is defended by the Black Knight. He asks the Black Knight to join his court at Camelot and to help in his quest for the Holy Grail. The Black Knight turns him down, so King Arthur begins to move by on his way across the bridge. The Black Knight finally speaks.

"None shall pass!"

"What?"

"None shall pass!"

King Arthur tries to reason with him.

"I have no quarrel with you good Sir Knight, but I must cross this bridge."

"Then you shall die!"

King Arthur is surprised but quickly turns indignant.

"I command you as King of the Britons to stand aside!"

The Black Knight stands his ground.

"I move for no man!"

Resolved to cross the bridge, King Arthur and the Black Knight become locked in deadly sword-to-sword combat. But the king gains the advantage by cutting off the Black Knight's left arm. Blood gushes out for a moment, but quickly subsides. The king assumes victory, but the Black

Knight refuses to yield.

"Tis but a scratch!"

"A scratch? Your arms off!"

"No it isn't!"

"Well, what's that then?"

"I've had worse."

"You lie."

"Come on you pansy!"

They continue to fight until the king hacks off the knight's other arm. The king assumes victory again, but the knight begins kicking him for all he's worth. King Arthur tries to convince him to stop, but the knight refuses to give up.

"It's just a flesh wound," he says.

The king is forced to cut off the Black Knight's right leg. The knight, undeterred, continues to hop on one leg and come at the king with head butts.

"Come here!"

"What are you going to do? Bleed on me?"

The knight replies.

"I'm invincible!

The left leg is hacked off and the Black Knight's torso and head plop onto the ground. The Black Knight looks up and says.

"All right. We'll call it a draw."

The king rides away with his servant as the Black Knight screams after him.

"Oh, I see. Running away? Come back here

and take what's coming to you! I'll bite your legs off!"

The silliness and comedy in this movie is a good illustration. The king wants the holy grail, that is, more wealth, more power, more control. In order to do that he has to defeat the citizen. The noble and powerful citizen must first be disarmed and then relegated to the lower status of subject to the ruling party.

But here is the crucial question, the one that's nagging like a splinter in my brain:

"If history can become legend, and legend become myth, is the reverse true?" Can myth become legend, and legend become history again? Can we regain our heritage? Can we take back that which was lost through complacency and lack of vigilance? And, more importantly, can it be done without the shedding of blood?

For our purposes, allow me to paraphrase Tolkien:

> *"And some things that should not*
> *have been forgotten were lost.*
> *History became legend. Legend*
> *became myth. And for two and*
> *a half thousand years, **freedom***
> *passed out of all knowledge."*

One of Ronald Reagan's most famous quotes is this:

> *"Freedom is never more than one*
> *generation away from extinction.*
> *We didn't pass it to our children in*
> *the bloodstream. It must be fought*
> *for, protected, and handed on for*
> *them to do the same."*

And that, my fellow Americans, is what the Second Amendment is all about. Live it, learn it, and pass the torch on to your children, lest tyranny overcome, and freedom pass out of all knowledge.

When tyranny tries to cross the bridge, the Second Amendment stands there unyielding, refusing to give way and cries out in a clarion voice:

THOU SHALL NOT PASS!

From the Founders

"A free people ought not only to be armed, but disciplined..."
– George Washington

"I prefer dangerous freedom over peaceful slavery."
– Thomas Jefferson

"What country can preserve its liberties if their rulers are not warned from time to time that their people preserve the spirit of resistance. Let them take arms."
– Thomas Jefferson

"They that can give up essential liberty to obtain a little temporary safety deserve neither liberty nor safety."
– Benjamin Franklin

"To disarm the people...is the most effectual way to enslave them."
– George Mason

"Before a standing army can rule, the people must be disarmed, as they are in almost every country in Europe.
– Noah Webster

Skip Coryell lives with his wife and children in Michigan. He is the author of *Concealed Carry for Christians* and *Civilian Combat: The Concealed Carry Book*. He is an avid hunter and sportsman, a Marine Corps veteran, and a graduate of Cornerstone University. You can listen to Skip as he co-hosts the syndicated military talk radio show *Frontlines of Freedom* on frontlinesoffreedom.com. You can also hear his weekly podcast *The Home Defense Show* at homedefense-show.com.

For more details on Skip Coryell, or to contact him personally, go to his website at skipcoryell.com.

Heller vs DC

In the landmark case heard by the US Supreme Court in 2008, the Second Amendment was upheld as an individual right to keep and bear arms. Prior to that, it was argued that the Second Amendment pertained only to the militia, which was being interpreted as the National Guard by anti-freedom advocates.

Despite this rebuke by the Supreme Court, anti-Second Amendment forces all across the country continue to chip away at the individual's right to keep and bear arms

"Eternal vigilance is the price of freedom."

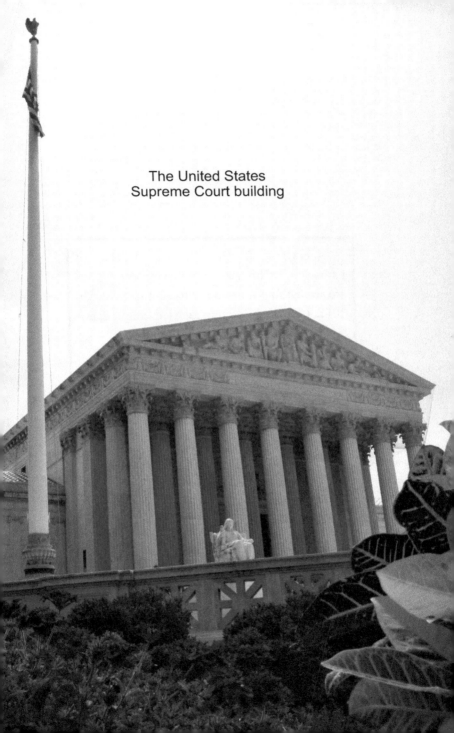

The United States
Supreme Court building

According to the National Center of Fathering, "Children in father-absent homes are almost four times more likely to be poor. In 2011, 12% of children in married-couple families were living in poverty, compared to 44% of children in mother-only families."

CHAPTER 3

FATHERLESS HOMES

BY MATT HAYES

THE UNITED STATES OF America is closing in on 144 years as a nation, and the country has grown more and progressed faster than any other culture in the history of the world. Our country is a Constitutional Republic and anchored by the ideas of liberty, freedom, justice, and individual rights and responsibilities. These core principles are unequivocally grounded in our founding documents: the Declaration of Independence, The United States Constitution and the Bill of Rights. Our particular brand of civilization has brought the world super sonic aircraft, the luxury automobile, advanced military equipment, flat screen TVs, cell phones, space travel, motion pictures, all kinds of music, art and literature, sports such as basketball, baseball and football, nuclear power, advanced medicines and many other accomplishments.

Any civilization or nation that wishes to maintain and cultivate a healthy, just, prosperous and sustainable society will have specific institutional needs in order to do so. Among the most important of these societal needs are safety, stability, law and order, natural resources, faith, education and freedom (just to name a few).

The family unit is by far the most important element in generating and achieving these societal benchmarks and is the building block upon which any civilization must depend. The family offers certain values and experiences to its members that are absolutely critical to the overall development of a thriving, safe and free society. An emotionally healthy family environment helps raise capable, intelligent, well-mannered and productive citizens dedicated to freedom and justice for all people. And as humans, we have a heart, soul and mind: therefore we need nurturing, acceptance, love, discipline and accountability in order to develop a proper sense of purpose for our lives.

Children raised in healthy traditional families normally derive this sense of purpose by acquiring principles and qualities from their parents such as civility, work ethic, compassion accountability, love, discipline, understanding, confidence, determination, courage and bravery. Contrary to what some may believe, children generally don't just develop these qualities on their own or in a 'parenting vacuum.' Human values must be intentionally taught by committed parents over the course of years as their children grow into adulthood. When instilled properly, these traits usually produce quality individuals who can contribute greatly to the ongoing development of their nation. And conversely, the evidence is extremely clear that when adults do not parent properly, their children may very well suffer serious issues such as anger, depression, suicidal thoughts, substance abuse, alcohol addiction, truancy, criminal activity, violent behavior, gang activity or sexual promiscuity. These behaviors and emotional issues can plague young people for many years, often leading to lack of education, broken relationships, loss of jobs, poverty, poor health, homelessness, arrest, incarceration, or suicide.

As these personal issues manifest in more and more individuals, they can become serious societal issues. In the last several generations our country has experienced a gradual and continuous breakdown of the family unit, leading to very deep cultural fissures and, for the first time, a regression in our overall national safety and prosperity. What would have, in the past, been considered both inconceivable and unacceptable in this country is now becoming normalized; a burgeoning number of homeless citizens, rampant drug use among younger adults, levels of marital divorce that are now in excess of 55%, the normalization of sexual promiscuity (with the resulting escalation in single motherhood and abortion) and an ever-increasing level of gang activity, opioid addiction and suicide. Not to mention the latest 'right' to be bestowed on our citizenry: the ability to choose and/or change one's human gender. Children as young as 7 years old are being encouraged to have gender-transition operations, at times against the wishes of one or even both of their parents.

How and why are such radical, harmful and perplexing changes being seen in our society in recent years? A big part of this cultural degradation emanates from the demise of the role of the father in America and the resulting disintegration of the nuclear family. The breakdown of the family is directly associated with the demise of fatherhood, and is being seen across all racial and socio-economic groups in the nation. But nowhere has this breakdown been more apparent than in African-American families. An examination of black communities in the 1940s, 50s and 60s would reveal strong family units living together,

supporting one another, building churches, founding businesses and maintaining a safe, functional
and vibrant culture; all while suffering systemic
racial discrimination and segregation. Honorable
men and women such as Martin Luther King Jr.,
Ella Baker, and James Lawson stepped forward
and began the civil rights movement, demanding
equality, justice and an end to Jim Crow laws for
the black community. This was an unbelievably
important step forward in the process of healing
and repairing the social fabric of this country.
Many positive things were happening back then,
but what does the black family look like today?!
We'll discuss that a bit later in this chapter.

Even though the mid-1960s ushered in the
official end of racial persecution and discrimination in America, radical and harmful ideologies
began to spread throughout the country as well.
Beginning at a grassroots level, and then ger-
minating on college campuses, these ideas were
aimed at normalizing selfish, indulgent attitudes
and behaviors. The mantra of peace, love, free sex
and drug experimentation spread quickly through
the younger generation, most notably among
young white men.

Around that same time the women's liberation
movement was getting into full swing, sending
American women the message that they should
be completely independent and never rely on any

man for their safety, security or future. This was the generation that had grown up in the tempestuous cauldron of the 1960s, marred by police brutality against civil rights groups, race riots, and growing disillusionment with the Vietnam war.

The changing societal norms as well as the welfare act of the mid-1960s both had a severe impact on personal behavior and, as a result, the nuclear American family. Early on, the deterioration of the family unit was most notable in the black community. By the mid 1970s a growing number of black fathers had abandoned their families, turning instead to a life of sexual promiscuity, alcoholism and drug addiction. The devastated families that were left behind turned to government welfare programs for basic assistance such as housing and food. Many black neighborhoods in urban areas became dangerously violent as drugs and prostitution became rampant. Over time, fatherless teens in these areas formed gangs for protection, acceptance and money.

The breakdown of the nuclear American family had accelerated at an alarming rate. In the almost 50 years since, the situation has only worsened. The epidemic of destruction has touched families across every racial group and reached all levels of financial income. Based on the social policies that have been espoused over this period of time, coupled with the complete lack of attention given to the breakdown of the traditional family unit, one might think that some powerful forces in this country have been directly intent on tearing at the very fabric that holds our society together. And all of us are starting to suffer because of it. Having stable, loving parents (especially fathers) in the home has historically been the single most important factor in raising physically and emotionally healthy children to contribute to the sustainability of our society. Good fathers spend time with their children, caring for them, teaching important life lessons, and ensuring that they learn discipline, hard work, concern for others, respect for authority, a sense of personal responsibility, and a thirst for knowledge and creativity that will lead them to a life well-lived!

Until the past few decades, fathers were universally responsible for the provision and safety of their families. As such they were irreplaceable in the social development of their children. The critical role of fatherhood does not in any way diminish or minimize the importance of a loving mother on the development of healthy children. However, empirical evidence overwhelmingly points to reliably involved fathers as the primary predictor of healthy families. Conversely, when fathers are absent from the home, children tend to experience significant levels of emotional instability. Be it acting out at school, behavioral issues at home, substance abuse or sexual activity, many children who grow up without a father experience significant social and/or emotional dysfunction. Despite this obvious connection, American pop culture portrays fathers as affable rubes who should be ridiculed more than revered and tolerated more than emulated. Increasingly, movies and music glorify rock stars and playboys instead committed, loving fathers; and idolize gang members and criminals rather than those who serve society like firemen and soldiers.

In major cities around the country, people in communities of color are being encouraged by their own elected officials to openly harass and defy authority. Instances of police and first-responders being ambushed, attacked and murdered have skyrocketed in recent years with no apparent response or remorse by the politicians and activists that perpetuate this violence. The most vilified group of people by social activists is now the middle-aged male tax payer. The message is becoming perfectly clear: men are the problem and traditional fatherhood is no longer valued but is instead mocked. All male authority figures, whether they be a CEO, policeman or politician are being vilified as oppressive and racist.

Sadly, this type of social engineering has been allowed to seep into our culture, and the impact on the traditional family has been catastrophic.

The complete reinvention of the family has produced incredible social problems in our society. Depression, anxiety, substance abuse and suicide are at epidemic levels across many demographics, but most profoundly seen in teens and young adults. ADHD and behavioral disorders are now considered the 'new normal' among American school children. Single motherhood is applauded as a brave and commendable pursuit. Dependence upon social welfare programs for housing, food, education and health care has spiraled upward to levels that are completely unsustainable. Let's be perfectly clear, though. Most of these issues are not new to us; they have existed for a very long time. But the alarming explosion in the numbers of people affected by these societal ills is very new and can be traced back directly and unequivocally to the breakdown of the traditional family.

Reinstituting traditional gender roles that were commonplace, let's say, in the 1950s is not necessarily the answer to our problems. However, a clear emphasis on the importance of the traditional family unit, with both the mother and father equally involved, is absolutely crucial to alleviating most of these troubling social issues facing our nation today.

Matt Hayes is a 1985 graduate of the United States Military Academy at West Point, and subsequently served as a Cavalry officer in cold-war West Germany. In addition to being an author, patriot and Gulf War combat veteran, he has worked as a medical sales professional for 20 years. Matt currently resides in Sarasota, Florida where he is active in his local community and volunteers in support of local veterans' groups.

From the Founders

The Founders sought to protect the traditional family in which a mother and father formed an affectionate union for better or worse and whose chief work was having and raising children. Marriage in the early republic took the idea of union seriously so that the marriage contract transcended the individualistic way of thinking that was characteristic of contracts. Lawmakers during the American Founding period, in keeping with the Western tradition of marriage, adopted coverture laws, which covered the wife under the legal identity of the husband, as a means used to protect this union,[6] though the common and municipal laws and the Founders' theory do not speak with one voice on the need for and depth of coverture to sustain the family's unity.

– Heritage Foundation

It is for freedom that Christ has set us free. Stand firm, then, and do not let yourselves be burdened again by a yoke of slavery.

Galatians 5:1 (NIV)

Now the Lord is the Spirit, and where the Spirit of the Lord is, there is freedom.

2 Corinthians 3:17 (NIV)

So if the Son sets you free, you will be free indeed.

John 8:36 NIV

I will walk about in freedom, for I have sought out your precepts.

Psalm 119:45 (NIV)

CHAPTER 4

WILL AMERICA ALWAYS CELEBRATE THE 4TH OF JULY?

BY PASTOR JEFF CARLSON

WHAT A BLESSING TO live in America! Like most amazing gifts given to us by the Lord, it is always possible to take our freedoms and liberties for granted and lose them amidst an often-unseen battle going on around us. As we stop on the 4th of July, we have many reasons to rejoice in the current progress for liberty and freedom for the Nation going on.

Recent, important decisions made by the Supreme Court have been very encouraging regarding the upholding of our Constitution and the cause of freedom. This constant battle for freedom has always been going on in every generation and was seen clearly by our Founding Fathers. Consider the following comments by some of the pillars of American liberty and freedom and their personal understanding of the great battle for freedom and liberty that is always underway.

John Adams - "You will never know how much it has cost my generation to preserve YOUR freedom. I hope you will make a good use of it."

Patrick Henry - "Is life so dear, or peace so sweet, as to be purchased at the price of chains and slavery? Forbid it, Almighty God! I know not what course others may take, but as for me, give me liberty or give me death!"

Thomas Jefferson - "The price of freedom is eternal vigilance."

Thomas Paine - "What we obtain too cheap, we esteem too lightly:

*it is dearness only that gives
everything its value. Heaven knows
how to put a proper price upon
its goods; and it would be strange
indeed if so celestial an article
as freedom should not be highly
rated."*

*Samuel Adams - "If ye love wealth
better than liberty, the tranquility of
servitude better than the animating
contest of freedom, go home from
us in peace. We ask not your
counsels or your arms. Crouch
down and lick the hands which feed
you. May your chains set lightly
upon you, and may posterity forget
that you were our countrymen."*

Many Americans have long understood that our freedoms must be vigorously defended in every generation. The moment one generation surrenders to the cultural sirens of slavery the Nation will begin fade away from the foundations of liberty without firing one shot. You see it is the quiet battles, that are ultimately spiritual in nature, that are always fought first. IF those battles are lost, the Nation will move toward slavery, tyranny and totalitarianism. As a result, it should be the goal of every freedom-loving American to speak up, vote and make sure that people are warned when such challenges to freedom arise from our own citizenry and government.

Back in 1776, around the time of our Nation's founding, a European historian, Alexander Fraser Tytler, published a work entitled, "The Decline and fall of the Athenian Republic." In his work, Tytler made the following observation:

A democracy cannot exist as a permanent form of government. It can only exist until the voters discover they can vote themselves largesse from the public treasury. From that moment on, the majority always votes for the candidates promising them the most benefits from the public treasury, with the result that a democracy always collapses over a loss of fiscal responsibility, always followed by a dictatorship. The average of the world's great civilizations before they decline has been 200 years. These nations have progressed in this sequence:

From bondage to spiritual faith,
From spiritual faith to great courage,
From courage to liberty,
From liberty to abundance,

From abundance to selfishness,
From selfishness to complacency,
From complacency to apathy,
From apathy to dependency,
From dependency back again to bondage.

As we look back on the last 243 years since our Nation was founded, we can begin to see America traveling down this same path of cultural decline. Perhaps the biggest sign of where we are right now is the rapid and rising growth of socialistic thinking among the electorate. The 2016 Presidential election marked the first time an avowed socialist, Senator Bernie Sanders, ran for the office. Since that time, we have been seeing a marked "mainstreaming" of socialistic thinking going on in our public square. Socialism is no longer for Europe or places like Venezuela; it is now seen as a viable option for a growing number of Americans. This rapid rise and growth of socialism is particularly strong among our young, especially our Millennial Generation, the largest American generation in history born between 1982 and 1996. In an article published by Bradford Richardson for the Washington Times on November 4, 2017, a poll was taken that revealed the following about what several of our Millennials seem to be thinking about socialism.

The majority of millennials would prefer to live in a socialist, communist or fascist nation rather than a capitalistic one, according to a new poll.

In the Victims of Communism Memorial Foundation's "Annual Report on U.S. Attitudes Toward Socialism," 58 percent of the up-and-coming generation opted for one of the three systems, compared to 42 percent who said they were in favor of capitalism.

The most popular socioeconomic order was socialism, with 44 percent support. Communism and fascism received 7 percent support each.

Marion Smith, executive director of the Victims of Communism Memorial Foundation, said the report shows millennials are "increasingly turning away from capitalism and toward socialism and even communism as a viable alternative."

"This troubling turn highlights widespread historical illiteracy in American society regarding socialism and the systemic failure of our education system to teach students about the genocide, destruction, and misery caused by communism since the Bolshevik Revolution one hundred years ago," Mr. Smith said in a statement.

The results of these polls should be a "wake up call" for every American that loves our Nation, freedoms and way of life. Sadly, our media, schools and culture are creating a "new" Nation before our eyes that has increasingly less and less to do with America as founded and understood in our Constitution. What the polls show us is that America is slowly, but surely, losing our ability to understand what happened on the 4th of July, 1776, and why it matters to every generation. As a new generation of socialistic thinking emerges, American freedoms will begin to die, and many won't even know what happened until it is too late. Americans may still have the 4th of July on the calendar and even shoot off some fireworks, but the real meaning of the holiday will be replaced with a revisionist meaning that has nothing in common with the original one.

Of course, the heart of our Nation's struggles with socialism has been as a result of drifting from the Lord Jesus Christ and the Christian Faith. After all, the rise of socialism reflects the loss of the Christian Faith and the void that is created when the Lord is gone. The rapid growth and control of the government over our lives is a barometer of what a society really wants to rule over them. Europe has already drifted into these socialistic patterns for a generation now and has ended up post-Christian in every case. America cannot be far behind based on what we are seeing now.

The spiritual principle and lesson of the hour is that no human system of government can rule over hearts, forgive sins or save souls. Real freedom and liberty come from the Lord alone. Only the Lord Jesus Christ can give us the deepest freedom we all need, a freedom from the bondage of sin and human government without God. That is the freedom our Lord talked about with the people of His day when He told them in John 8:31-36,

To the Jews who had believed him, Jesus said, "If you hold to my teaching, you are really my disciples. Then you will know the truth, and the truth will set you free." They answered him, "We are Abraham's descendants and have never been slaves of anyone. How can you say that we shall be set free?" Jesus replied, "Very truly I tell you, everyone who sins is a slave to sin. Now a slave has no permanent place in the family, but a son belongs to it forever. So, if the Son sets you free, you will be free indeed."

On this 242nd anniversary of our Nation's founding, the Gospel message is still the Good News for any individual and/or society. One simply cannot remove God from any society and remain free. The Founders of this Nation understood that powerful truth from the beginning. When the Lord is our Lord and when our sins are forgiven we are a truly free people. When we know the Lord, we have found the true Government we all are looking for in this life and the world to come. Real freedom is living out the Christian life each day and enjoying the Lord forever. Such truth always leads to praise, worship and thanksgiving of which fireworks is but a small witness on the 4th of July. Let's all run to Jesus as our King and celebrate our glorious freedoms in Him alone.

> *Pastor Jeff Carlson is Skip Coryell's pastor and Denny Gillem's friend. Jeff had the idea of this book. He is the only contributor to this book who did not serve in the US military. However, Jeff is certainly a warrior in God's army and is passionate about our nation.*

From the Founders

"Well, Doctor, what have we got—a Republic or a Monarchy?"

"A Republic, if you can keep it."
— Benjamin Franklin at the close of the Constitutional Convention of 1787.

A constitutional republic is a state where the chief executive and representatives are democratically elected by the people, and the rules are set down in a written constitution. The head of state and other representatives are elected but they do not have uncontrolled power. What they may do is written in the constitution. If there is dispute about what the constitution means, this is decided by a court which is independent from the politicians.

The constitution describes how the state may be run. The constitution limits the power of each officeholder. Constitutional republics usually have a separation of powers. The separation of powers means that no single officeholder gets unlimited power. John Adams said that a constitutional republic was "a government of laws, and not of men." Constitutional governance argue is meant to be a safeguard against tyranny. No office holder can get to a position of absolute power. Aristotle was the first to write about the idea in his works on politics.

Jeff Carlson was born in Illinois and raised in the Chicago suburbs. Jeff came to personal faith in the Lord Jesus Christ as a college freshman through the witness of a campus evangelist. He graduated from the University of Illinois in Urbana, Illinois with a degree in engineering and worked in the corporate world for several years before his call to ministry.

Following graduation from Fuller Theological Seminary in Pasadena, California Jeff came to Oakhill Church in Grand Rapids, Michigan where he currently serves as pastor.

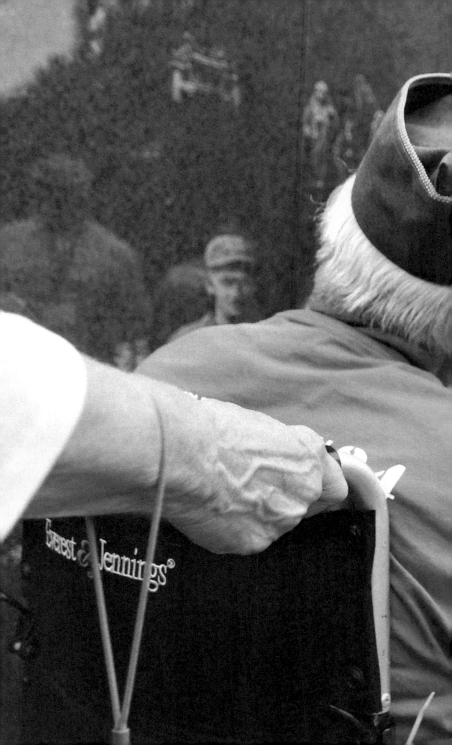

An old warrior visits his fallen comrades at the Korean War Memorial Wall. The spiritual bond between soldiers is infinite and never fading. It is a bond of the deepest and strongest kind ... a bond of unseen blood.

> *Borders are to distinct countries*
> *what fences are to neighbors: means*
> *of demarcating that something on*
> *one side is different from what lies*
> *on the other side.*
>
> — *Denny Gillem*

CHAPTER 5

OUR SOUTHERN BORDER

BY JOHN MURRAY

A FEW MONTHS AGO I SAW A TELE-vision commentary by Democrat leaders, Speaker Pelosi and Senator Schumer, after they had indicated a willingness to negotiate wall funding with President Trump, following several weeks of sparring. Instead of reasonable, respectful discussion, they stressed that the president had manufactured a crisis at the border, and that they would offer only a small pittance of support. I was flabbergasted in my disbelief that they could be so mendacious as to say there was no problem and not admit the multitude of incursions and infractions in the US/Mexican border area.

How could they not be aware of the great quantities of illegal border crossings, the drug trafficking, the danger to Americans living in isolated areas in the vicinity, the idiocy of sanctuary states and cities who protect illegal criminals with multiple deportations and kill innocent Americans (Kate Steinle and others), the huge costs involved and on and on?

But I do understand the situation - their politics are more important to them than their country! And, those with Trump Derangement Syndrome (TDS - my definition: a sickness of the head caused by extreme hate for Trump which induces rage and precludes logical thought) are beyond hope of self-controlled decorum.

Although I knew I would be spinning my wheels, I decided to write my congressman (a Democrat, of course, here in super liberal Northern Virginia) to point out that there is a significant number of his constituents who don't agree with his blind support of the speaker. He replied a month or so later (a missive obviously written by a staffer) with a lesson on how important immigrants have been in the history of our country, etc., etc., etc. I guess I should have told him that I was the grandson of Irish immigrants. And, of course, the letter included some criticisms of the president.

Our liberal media and politicians try to lead us to believe that there is no problem on our southern border. Previous presidents, including Clinton and Obama, on occasion did acknowledge such, although Obama later on refused the invitation of the Governor of Texas to visit it, saying it was not important (or words to that effect).

As I mentioned earlier, the politics of the losing Democrats (diversity and climate change) still prevail for them, whereas the winning Republicans are still stressing national security and the economy. I personally have a hard time understanding the minds of liberals. Before going into some significant details of our southern border, I would like to relate an encounter I had in the Fairfax County Juvenile and Domestic Relations Court's Volunteer Interpreter Office (where I have volunteered for more than twenty-two years since there aren't enough certified (salaried) Spanish interpreters to handle the ever-increasing workload).

A few days before the midterm elections in, November 2018, as three others and I were about to depart at the end of the day, one of them (a Latina who had acquired her US citizenship) firmly stated, "We must vote!" She then turned to me and asked, "Are you going to vote?" I replied, "Yes, even though my conservative vote here in Liberal Land won't mean anything, I will do my civic duty and vote." She looked me in the eye and queried, " Are you a conservative?" I said, "Yes." Her reply: "You can't be a conservative! Because

if you were, you wouldn't be here helping people."
I just chuckled and stated, "I know your source
of information." It goes to show that the liberal
media mislead our gullible population.

Brainwashing, perhaps?

After the Mexican-American War (1846 -
1848) the US acquired Texas, California, Nevada,
Utah, New Mexico, most of Arizona and Colorado
and parts of Oklahoma, Kansas and Wyoming,
resulting in the territorial size of Mexico being
cut in half. In the early 1900's tensions along the
border started to rise and fences began being built.
By the 1990's the number of migrants continued to
increase as the patchwork system of border crossings, flimsy walls and wire fences, open spaces,
deserts and urban areas provided inadequate security along the almost 2,000 mile border.

The Secure Fence Act of 2006 provided for 700
miles of high-security fencing in heavily transited
areas. The result was that incursions were funneled
into more rural, dangerous spaces and migrant
deaths greatly increased due to harsh terrain and
extreme temperatures. Some remains were discovered years later but some will never be found. By
2010 the fencing initiative was terminated for being over budget, full of glitches and behind sched-
ule. Subsequently, the number of incursions and
apprehensions began to rise significantly, along
with increased violence and drug trafficking.

Concurrently, a humanitarian crisis has developed due to a shortage of resources that especially affect migrant children. Needless to say, the related facilities and border patrol have become overwhelmed with the increased number of migrants (our southern border is the most frequently crossed border in the world with almost 350 million documented crossings annually (half a million of which are illegals) during the past three decades). In addition, there are an estimated 70,000 - 80,000 undetected crossers each year who disappear into the interior or die. As such, there are numerous humanitarian assistance groups which provide shelters, water and medical services throughout the border zone (up to 100 miles on each side of the border). As these problems continue to snowball, the overworked personnel of the Border Patrol, ICE (Immigration and Customs Enforcement) and other agencies of the Department of Homeland Security undeservedly suffer the politically-motivated criticism of our liberal politicians and media. Also under constant fire from this unworthy opposition is President Trump, who considers this issue to be a potential threat to our national security. After observing the immigration happenings in Europe during recent years (rapidly increasing population (mostly Muslim), demands ("No Go" zones. Sharia Law, significant welfare costs et.al.), rising crime rates and a host of other negative factors) I have to agree with our president. By striving to enhance our border security, he has the protection of the American people at heart, not his political party.

Liberals are saying that enhancing the wall is too expensive and not worth the effort. Consider what our tax money is currently providing for illegals. The numbers are astounding!

$538.3 Billion a year for the following:

- welfare, Medicaid, education, incarceration (approximately 20% of all federal inmates are illegal aliens from Latin America), deportation, suppressed American wages and other associated costs).

President Trump's requested $12.8 Billion for the next budget's border security included a physical barrier, law enforcement (additional Border Patrol agents and immigration lawyers) and humanitarian priorities. That would result in being a small fraction of what would be saved by the reduction of the recent rampant illegal immigration.

Other important benefits would include:

- a much smaller crime rate which would lessen the fear factor of death, accidents, rapes and other crimes by illegals

- additional federal (and state, city and local) income taxes would be collected because fewer people would be working "off the books,"

- overcrowded schools would save billions in ESL and free breakfasts and lunches
- Americans wouldn't suffer thousands of TB and hepatitis cases brought in by illegals unscreened at our border
- our cities would see much fewer people driving and polluting.

And, speaking of our cities, the addition of illegals is exacerbating the already disastrous situation in Los Angeles, San Francisco and other liberal West Coast cities which are beset with human waste and drug paraphernalia in their streets. The list keeps going!

It won't be easy, but our Department of Homeland Security is striving to clean up the debacle of our southern border. Improved wall construction is a long-range project which will require congressional cooperation (not a given) and presidential leadership (i.e., re-election of Donald Trump). Just recently the administration announced an end to the "catch and release" policy (the practice of arresting border crossers then immediately releasing them into the community). Families that attempt to claim asylum will usually be sent to wait in Mexico while their cases proceed in US immigration courts. Those who don't attempt to claim asylum will be quickly returned to their home countries. The Department of Homeland Security has laid the groundwork for El

Salvador, Guatemala and Honduras to cooperate with Mexico in this endeavor.

Dealing with the liberals in our congress and a maniacal media makes progress difficult, but fortunately we have some persistent patriots who realize the importance of a secure southern border.

Besides the challenge of our own internal dissent, there has recently emerged the tactic of using the internet for human smuggling. Details for off the books driving are posted by WhatsApp or Snapchat, and drivers earn good money by making a pickup near the border and dropping off further north, into the interior. Truck drivers also can seek this opportunity as evidenced not long ago by a tractor-trailer with 53 illegals that was stopped at a Texas highway checkpoint. The driver claimed he didn't know how they got in his truck but his cell phone had the evidence.

For the time being, the United States sits on top of a complicated world with many countries laden with many problems. We have our share of them here. Unfortunately, one of the most serious is the wide political divide that seems to have widened since the 2016 election, which so greatly shocked the losing liberals. As a consequence, they are determined to thwart the president at every opportunity and are driven by their hate for him to such a degree that they would be happy to see our country fail if such would take him down. This attitude

(TDS for the most fanatical) is highly detrimental to accomplishing many governmental missions, one of which is improved security of our southern border.

Also affected is civility within our population at different levels, including within families. One relative, in a heated discussion with my wife (who was outnumbered three to one) screamed at her, "What's wrong with you military people?"

What a shame! That attitude could elicit another chapter in this book!

The bottom line is this:

> *For the benefit of the American people and those attempting to enter our country, we must continue striving to overcome the hurdles in our border security path, to include weeding out undesirables.*

One of my good Latin American friends achieved his US citizenship after seven years of properly going through the process and has been a successful civil engineer and a proud American. Let's welcome the worthy and turn away those not so.

From the Colonel

Western rules that promote a greater likelihood of consensual government, religious tolerance, an independent judiciary, free-market capitalism, and the protection of private property combine to offer the individual a level of prosperity and personal security rarely enjoyed at home. As a result, migrants make the necessary travel adjustments to go westward — especially given that Western civilization, uniquely so, has usually defined itself by culture, not race, and thus alone is willing to accept and integrate those of different races who wish to share its protocols.

Borders are to distinct countries what fences are to neighbors: means of demarcating that something on one side is different from what lies on the other side. Borders amplify the innate human desire to own and protect property and physical space, which is impossible to do unless it is seen — and can be so understood — as distinct and separate. Clearly delineated borders and their enforcement, either by walls and fences or by security patrols, won't go away because they go to the heart of the human condition — what jurists from Rome to the Scottish Enlightenment called *meum et tuum*, mine and yours. Between friends, unfenced borders enhance friendship; among the unfriendly, when fortified, they help keep the peace.

John Murray, a retired Army colonel and university Spanish professor, is a 1964 graduate of West Point and holds masters degrees from Middlebury College and Long Island University. During his Army career he served as a Field Artillery Officer and a Latin American Foreign Area Officer and was assigned duty on four continents. He currently resides with his wife, Louise, in Northern Virginia.

WILLIAM L LUTZ

• RODNEY H M

MICHAEL J MIT

MICHA

• RAYMOND F

There are 58,320 names on the Vietnam
Memorial wall, but each name represents an
American military veteran who honorably
served America. Each name is special. Each
name is loved, honored and revered.

ARTHUR E SCOTT

• NATH

• JAMES V SP

ROBERT D L

ADANO HERNE

UNAKEA • JOSE

ELL • WAVERY M

OSEPH P McKN

S O'BRIEN • TIM

ORVELL • MARV

RION D POWEL

BERT A ROOSSIE

ALD M SET

MONS

There are important events in each of our lives, dates on which things happened which made an important impact on our lives and who we are as people. Certainly, birth and graduations and marriages and awards are some of those. It's good to look at your life and identify the key events that made a positive impact on your life and, in one way or another, celebrate them. This helps us understand, counsel, and/ or mentor others. It also gives us something to look at when we need introspection. Certainly, service to our nation and to our local communities provide many of those occasions. We salute those who served our nation honorably, and we don't forget those who serve in a thousand ways in our local communities.

CHAPTER 6

ANNIVERSARIES

BY BOB ANDERSON

FOR MOST PEOPLE, THE word anniversary has a singular meaning: the day of your birth; the day you graduated from high school and for some the day you graduated from college. Other days ring the same generally happy thoughts: the day of your wedding; the birth of your children; your first hard-earned promotion at work. There are sad dates too: the death of your parents; the difficult loss of a child or a spouse.

Soldiers have these same anniversary dates plus a few more: the day you went into the service and the day you left active duty. It's those in-between dates that I would like to reflect on here.

In my case, after a less than stellar first attempt to matriculate from Michigan State University, I decided to enlist into the Regular Army. The early spring of 1968 brought forth the usual and highly anticipated cherry blossoms to Washington, DC, where I lived as an Air Force brat, with my parents and younger sister. I had enlisted in Alexandria, VA, so I was sent to Richmond for my pre-induction physical and testing on 4 April 1968. To many, even now, that date doesn't immediately conjure up any significance. It was, however, a seminal moment in our nation's history, because on that day, the Reverend Doctor Martin Luther King Jr was assassinated in Memphis.

On our way back to Washington, in the early evening hours, we could see from our Greyhound bus, that Washington was literally ablaze. I was fortunate to catch a ride on the last bus out of the District that evening, and was dropped off at the first stop in College Park, Maryland. A wide spot in the road defined a bus stop, and I was ever hopeful that my father would shortly arrive to pick me up. His timing was perfect, and he arrived with my mother and sister after only a few anxious minutes. I still remember that on the front seat of the family car, he had his .32 Caliber Smith & Wesson Colt Pistol, just in case.

The next meaningful date occurred after another bus ride back to Richmond where I was formally inducted into the United States Army on my mother's birthday – May 6th. After a box lunch we were taken by train to Columbus, GA and then bussed to the Army Reception Station at Fort Benning. I had arrived!

For decades Fort Benning has been training soldiers in the art of warfare, and my training was basically the same as those soldiers who fought their way across Europe, the Pacific and later Korea. We were (and still are) the Infantry – the Queen Of Battle, We Infantry, for hundreds of years, have been the first to storm the fortresses of our respective enemies. That was our job in 1776 and remains so to this very day. To close with and (in up close and often personal circumstances) vanquish those that stand in our way! To compound the angst many of us felt when Dr, King was killed in April, along came June 6th and the assassination of Robert Kennedy in Los Angeles.

I graduated from Basic Combat Training in July of 1968 as an 11B10, Infantryman. Our brigade commander called us "Soldiers," which was a welcoming word from Trainee and other more descriptive and vile words. That was a glorious day in our lives and afterward, our company scattered to the various parts of the United States to begin our next phase of learning the idiosyncrasies of soldiering.

About twelve of us were sent to Fort Dix, NJ – Home of The Ultimate Weapon – for further training in the skills necessary to become that weapon. Classes in Radio Telephone procedures; qualification on the M16 Rifle; M60 Machine Gun; 3.5-Inch Rocket Launcher; the M18-A1 Anti-Personnel (Claymore) Mine; the .50 Caliber M2 Heavy Browning Machine Gun; First Aid; Drill and Ceremony. We bivouacked under the stars, took long walks with heavy packs and did thousands of push-ups for minor infractions. We were also trained in crowd control, for possible duty in Philadelphia, which was the closest big city, because of the high state of civil unrest in our great country during this, the summer of 1968.

I had qualified through testing in Richmond to attend Officer Candidate School, and I gladly accepted the Army's offer, and, after a short visit back home, again found myself at Fort Benning to attend the 23-week course leading to a Reserve Commission as a 2nd Lieutenant of Infantry. Classes were like those at Forts Benning and Dix but were much more intensely focused. Our job, should we graduate, would be that of a rifle company platoon leader in the faraway place called the Republic of South Vietnam. Most of us had no inkling of what was going to happen after graduation ... myself included. Although I was the son of a career United States Air Force pilot, their job is quite a bit different from a mud-slogging, C-Ration-eating infantry soldier.

I graduated on 29 March 1969, and along with about 90 other classmates, began the next phase of our Army careers. I stayed at Fort Benning for about 5 months until receiving orders to Vietnam. This is what I had been trained for and I was not at all apprehensive. That assignment was to be the grand adventure of my life, and I was truly looking forward to it. I believed all the talk of the Domino Theory that millions of us had been exposed to, but that would change in the stinking jungles of South Vietnam and Cambodia.

I arrived in Vietnam in October of 1969 after a 2+ week delay en route excursion to Fort Sherman's Jungle Operation School. After a few days of acclimation and orientation at Bien Hoa's, 90th Replacement Battalion, I was assigned to the 1st Air Cavalry Division (Airmobile) and further assignment to George Custer's 7th Cavalry. I flew to the brigade base camp, Quan Loi, on a C-7A Caribou. Quan Loi was just a few miles from the provincial capital called An Loc, which in 1973 became a pivotal battle between the Army of South Vietnam and the North Vietnamese Army. That however was down a long and winding road strewn with the bodies of many soldiers, both friend and foe!

Infantry Combat as previously alluded to is up close and personal. Two opposing sides desperately trying to kill each other often at distances less than 75 feet. It's not a clean environment at all: dirty; stinking, bloody and horrific. This was and continues to this day to be the job of the Infantry – close with an enemy, seize the ground and vanquish those that lay before us. Because if we didn't, they would do it to us! Warfare isn't pretty, and if you don't have the stomach for it, don't take up the challenge.

On 3 December 1969, 4,000 meters west of Fire Support Base Jerri, in III Corps, my rifle platoon was leading our company in the all-consuming search for the enemy. We crossed a well-used trail and set up, then I called the company commander forward for consultation. A few minutes later, two NVA soldiers appeared suddenly to my front. In a scene reminiscent of the OK Corral, I was able to shoot first and two enemy combatants lay dead on the ground. In these types of situations, you react to the threat, because there isn't time to give much thought other than – it's them or me! As this was late in the afternoon, we had been left behind to see if any more NVA might appear, perhaps looking for the NVA major who lay just 30 feet from us.

Toward dusk, we spotted about 30 enemy soldiers crossing to our front about 400 meters away as we lay well hidden behind a couple of big logs. They were too far to effectively engage with our platoon weapons, so I called in an Artillery Fire Mission, COBRA Helicopter Gunships and USAF Tac Air onto that column. When the smoke had cleared and the noise had abated, 28 more NVA soldiers lay dead!

This incident has stayed with me for almost 50 years for many reasons: in his personal belongings, this enemy soldier (a major) carried a photo of himself, his wife and daughter. They would never know that their loved one died on a stinking, hot and humid day because an American infantry 2nd lieutenant was quicker to shoot. I am still dealing with this event because "Thou Shall Not Kill," is a commandment in the Bible.

On 26 April 1970, just before the 'official' entry of United States Forces into the Kingdom of Cambodia, my 2nd company became involved in another firefight. We were still in III Corps, but now 4,000 meters east of Firebase Frances. The company commander was killed along with another Sky Trooper. As I was dealing with artillery, gunship and medevac assets, I watched our medics desperately trying to save this wounded soldier, all the while under fire! A bit later as the incoming fire dwindled to a few shots now and again, my platoon sergeant and I crawled out and recovered the body of our commander. That recovery sent him home to Chicago and into the shattered lives of his family. A few years ago, I had the opportunity to tell his oldest son that his dad died bravely, and he did not suffer. On that date, we had two Sky Troopers killed and 18 wounded, including me.

On 29 April 1970, the Lieutenant that had replaced me in Alpha Company was killed just 2,000 meters, NE of our battle on the 26th.

My adopted Company lost five killed from my old platoon on 17 May 1970 and just a week later, four friends from the 1st platoon were killed. These brave soldiers fought and died in Cambodia. In June another soldier was killed, yet even after heroic effort and more casualties in an attempt at recovery, his body had to be left behind.

There were many other events that I and others shared during my combat tour but these represent what most infantry soldiers endured. No amount of training can prepare a person for this type of life-changing event. It's called post traumatic stress for a reason!

Perhaps you have heard the term PTSD or as it's now referred to as PTS? In 2005, I was diagnosed with almost all those symptoms, just as hundreds of thousands who have gone before me. A triggering event, which exacerbates the symptoms, most often sneaks up on us when we least expect it. It can come from a helicopter flying overhead, a whiff of diesel fuel, or an Oldie but Goodie playing on the radio. Many of us are also easily startled: cars backfiring; someone dropping a table behind us on a concrete floor, July 4th fireworks, especially. It doesn't take much, really, to bring back all the heartache and angst.

My generation of veteran was vilified by many when we returned from our war. It was an unpopular situation based upon faulty intelligence and orchestrated by Robert McNamara. My father flew many of those architects from Andrews, AFB, to Saigon and around the world as a command pilot in the 89th Military Airlift Wing. He once flew President Thieu and Vice Premier Ky from Saigon to Guam to confer with President Johnson on how next to prosecute the war. I think that was in 1967.

After active duty, I returned to Michigan State University, graduating in 1974 with a BA in General Business and in 1976 with an MBA in Personnel Management. My working career, like many of my generation, was sometimes governed by baggage from our war. Not knowing the whys, that baggage lead to inappropriate behavior at work: snapping at co-workers, becoming frustrated with superiors, etc. These and other behaviors caused me to eventually move on in the continuing search for a perfect job. The three positive constants however were my wife, Julie, and our daughter, Rebecca, and my sister, Susan.

All three standing beside me through the bad but mostly good times!

I have been active for 40+ years in helping veterans achieve what they deserve from the Veterans Administration. I have been decorated for heroism and wounded in ground combat, but for me my proudest achievements, outside of my family, have come from the work that I have done with the Kent County Veterans Honor Guard, my recognition as the 2019 Veteran of the Year from the United Veterans Council of Kent County, and my selection this year as the President Emeritus of the 7th United States Cavalry Association. These awards and accolades would never have come my way had I not taken the oath in May of 1968!

Our veterans have served honorably and sacrificed so much, as did those family members who were left behind. We have a sacred duty to honor the memory of our brothers and sisters who fell then and who still fall today, to ensure that their sacrifice WAS. NOT. IN. VAIN!

Not a day goes by without my thinking of those lives lost, of my friends who died, helping to keep the dream of a free nation alive. These sobering reminders are referred to as survivor's guilt, and thousands of veterans suffer from the

American Military Veterans

"Why Them and Not Me?"

So, there you have it: anniversary dates from the soul of a Combat Infantry Lieutenant, both the good and the not so good that a war veteran experiences, sometimes every day.

May God continue to bless the United States!

Important Dates
From the Founders

December 16, 1773 - "Boston Tea Party" takes place as residents disguised as Indians throw crates of tea into Boston Harbor.

April 19, 1775 - Revolutionary War officially begins with the Battles of Lexington and Concord.

June 14, 1775 - Continental Army established by the Continental Congress.

September 25, 1789 - US Congress adopts the Bill of Rights (containing the 1st 10 Amendments) and sends it to the states to be ratified.

September 20, 1814 - "Star-Spangled Banner" written.

July 4, 1776 - US declares its Independence from Britain as Congress approved the Declaration of Independence).

June 21, 1788 - United States Constitution goes into effect after the necessary 9 states have ratified it.

November 11, 1918 - Allied and Central Powers sign an armistice, ending World War I -- Was Armistice Day; now Veterans Day

September 2, 1945 - Japan unconditionally surrenders to the United States, ending World War II.

American Military Veterans

1969 on FSB Jerri, in III Corps

Bob Anderson enlisted in the United States Army in May of 1968. After Basic and AIT, he attended Infantry Officer Candidate School at Fort Benning, and graduated as a 2nd Lieutenant on March 29th, 1969. He arrived in Vietnam in October of 1969 and was assigned as a Platoon Leader in the 1st Battalion, 7th Cavalry. He received two Bronze Star's for Valor and an Army Commendation Medal for Valor along with a Purple Heart. Active in Veteran's Issues for 40 years he is the current Kent County Veteran of the Year, as recognized by the United Veterans Council of Kent County (MI), the current Commander of the Kent County Veterans Honor Guard, where he has done over 980 veteran funerals. This year as recognition for his many years of service to the 7th Cavalry Association, he was elected President Emeritus.

Arlington National Cemetery

Arlington officially became a national cemetery on June 15, 1864, by order of Secretary of War Edwin Stanton. Initially, the cemetery was only 200 acres in size, but since has grown substantially. Presently the cemetery is 639 acres, and is the final resting place for over 400,000 active duty service members, veterans and their families.

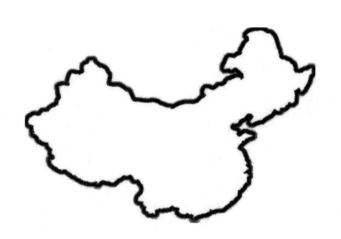

CHAPTER 7

CHINA'S PRIME TARGET

BY TOM ANTHONY

DRIVING ALONG THE Pacific Coast Highway from our home in Huntington Beach to the Veterans Hospital for my annual exam, I passed, on my left, a US Navy vessel docked at Seal Beach, and, on my right, thousands of acres of bunkers storing naval weapons. Mobile cranes loading heavy ammo onto the docked warships made me think if China were to go to war with the US the Seal Beach Naval Weapons Station would have to be China's Prime Target.

My life has had some elements of fighting windmills, always on a journey to the next place, the meadow on the other side of the hill. I enjoy continuing my personal journey but fear the journey my country has embarked upon.

Our military power has no effect on the agenda of the Islamic states. Oil prices crashing will make Iran and Russia find new directions on their journeys while Americans max out their credit cards shopping for Christmas presents made in China.

The Chinese military is modernizing and focused on an objective. The US as a nation has no clear global objective, and for years has been getting involved in nations we do not understand and trying to draw borders. China has global objectives starting in the South China Sea, has achieved stalemate with Russia, but has few overseas military outposts encroaching onto the domain of other nations.

A primary objective of China into the future is control of the South China Sea (the Philippine Sea) where the United States conducts joint military operations with the Armed Forces of the Philippines, South Korea, and with other countries.

How would the US react if China formed alliances with Canada and Mexico and conducted joint exercises on US borders? China has a military base in Djibouti – big deal, and has conducted exercises with Russia – there's a bigger message! Chinese military power is near that of the US and is becoming aggressive in the seas surrounding the Philippines, the oldest and closest US ally in Asia.

Supporting the military, China's strategy to rival the US in world influence is unfair economics. Economics 101 is based on laws such as the Theory of Competitive Advantage and the Law of Supply and Demand. A simple example of Competitive Advantage: it is more efficient to grow bananas in the Philippines than in Korea and it is more efficient to manufacture computers in Korea than in the Philippines. Assume one person can grow 1,000 bananas per day in the Philippines and one person can make 1 computer per day in Korea. Yes, bananas could be grown in Korea in a greenhouse, but at great expense. And computers could be made in the Philippines but at greater cost due to lack of infrastructure.

Pretend that bananas sell for 1 peso each in the Philippines and computers in Korea for 1,000 won. Trade would benefit both countries if they trade 1,000 bananas for 1 computer. Both parties win.

The Central Banks could let rates float, and, according to the laws of supply and demand, the exchange rate could settle at the exchange rate in 1 won equals 1000 pesos. All is fair.

But what if a country decides to manipulate the exchange rate? The Central Bank of Korea increases the value of the won to 2,000 pesos and exchanges only at that rate? A customer in Korea still pays 1,000 won for a computer but now for 1,000 won he can import 2,000 bananas instead of only 1,000.

A customer in the Philippines could still import a computer but now has to pay 2,000 pesos for it because the value of the peso had been reduced by the action of the Korean Central Bank. The demand for computers in the Philippines would decrease and the demand for bananas in Korea would increase as the price has fallen in half.

Therefore, Korea would create wealth from un-fair trade with the Philippines. This wealth could be transferred from Korea back to the Philippines at artificially favorable rates for the won. Korean enterprises could gain control of land and busi-nesses in the Philippines cheaply, paid for by the money printed by their Central Bank.

Consider a real example, not the silly, hypo-thetical one above. China sets the exchange rate for their currency and exports products to the USA, selling below the cost to manufacture in the USA. The dollars the Chinese receive they use to buy land and factories in the USA, which they will own … forever.

American Military Veterans

After a war without objective in Vietnam, fighting a useless war in an impoverished third world country that would one day become an ally against the real threat to the USA, China, I got my first real job, in international business with Firestone, at that time an American company. At a meeting of the US Tire and Rubber industry in Washington DC in 1984, I had a glass of wine standing in a small circle with the Presidents of Goodyear, Firestone, General and Goodrich. Today only Goodyear is a US company. My company was put out of business by high quality and lower priced Chinese imports.

Today I see MRF tires from India, Kumho from Korea, many brands from Japan, and several brands made in China. When I worked for Firestone and went to the Philippines doing strategic planning and global marketing in 1981, our factory in Manila operated at capacity and Firestone had over 30% local market share. Now that factory is closed, the Firestone brand does not exist in the market and continues in the US only as one of the brands owned by Bridgestone.

I moved to the consumer electronics business. Zenith was purchased by a Japanese company and moved from Chicago to Mexico under a different name. In the lobby of the Japan Victrola Corporation (JVC) in Tokyo I saw the iconic statue of that puppy listening to a Victrola, once the famous image of the Radio Corporation of America (RCA).

Profits in Japan, Korea and China are used to invest in their infrastructure and also returned to the US as they buy real estate. The US allows foreigners to own real estate; China does not. Real estate prices in the US have increased dramatically, homes are often too expensive for middle class Americans.

In 2011, General Electric, one of the oldest, biggest, most All- American of companies, moved its hundred-year old X-ray operation from Wisconsin to Beijing, China. In addition to moving the headquarters, the company invested $2 billion to build research centers to train Chinese engineers with US technology. How's GE stock doing today?

"Pedros" who have accompanied America on our quixotic journey – like Australia, Britain, Japan, Canada and the Philippines – get few rewards while hostility has few consequences. Instead we court Turkey and threaten Iran. The United States does not have the will nor the assets required to keep the Philippines independent of China.

Chaos in the world. People forget the lessons of history and repeat mistakes that destroy humanity. And things are different now. Wars could be nuclear. The US has the weapons, many "nukes" stored at the Seal Beach Naval Weapons Station in California.

The Philippines could crash and become a part of China. President Duterte is right, make peace with China and no need for US noses pushed in trying to manage it. (We have enough going on in other places – with little success.) So what now? The overpowering Chinese are on the doorstep and smell the oil under the South China Sea. The United States is locked into a new Cold War. Hence my first Novel, *Rebels of Mindanao*, evolved, asking the question, what would happen if the rebels won? Would the USA become deeply involved in another war? Could the USA wage war on two fronts?

The United States government owes what amounts to everything earned by everyone in the country for a year to China. China gave the cash from the profits they made when they sold us their stuff back to us to hold for them. Now they hold pieces of paper that say, "We promise to pay…" What if we do not pay them back and declare the paper worthless? China will retaliate, make the Philippines part of "Greater China" and expropriate the US factories and property in China.

While we ride an old horse and carry a broken lance, China is rising. We cannot fight a war in the South China Sea and win. We have to fight a war we can win or our nation will continue its decline.

Thus, there is no reason for China to attack the Seal Beach Naval Weapons Station; they are already winning the bigger war.

The US economy is China's Prime Target.

Anthony holds the BS degree in engineering from the US Military Academy, West Point NY and the MBA in International Business from the University of Akron. Anthony also did doctoral work at the University of Vienna, Austria.

Anthony, a Ranger and combat veteran awarded the Purple Heart, Bronze Star, and Air Medal among other awards, remains active in community service, working with US Congressmen to appoint candidates to the US Military Academy. He is a Past President of the West Point Alumni of Northern Ohio.

Tom Anthony studied creative writing for three years at the University of California. He is the author of several novels and screenplays including the Amazon best-seller, *Rebels of Mindanao*, *Sabine*, *Warsaw Triple Cross* and *Sarangani Girl*.

Frontlines of Freedom

China

A Socialist State, the People's Republic of China, is a country in East Asia and is the world's most populous country, with a population of around 1.428 billion in 2017. Covering approximately 3,700,000 square miles; it is the third- or fourth-largest country by area. It is governed by the Communist Party of China,

China emerged as one of the world's first civilizations, in the fertile basin of the Yellow River in the North China Plain. For millennia, China's political system was based on hereditary monarchies, or dynasties. When the Republic of China replaced the Qing dynasty, China was ravaged by feudal warlordism and Japan during WWII. The subsequent Chinese Civil War in 1949 was when the Communist Party of China led by Mao Zedong established the People's Republic of China.

China is a unitary one-party socialist republic and is one of the few existing socialist states. Political dissidents and human rights groups have denounced the Chinese government for human rights abuses, mass surveillance, and cracking down on protests.

The Chinese government says that the right to subsistence and economic development is a prerequisite to other types of human rights, and that the notion of human rights should take into account a country's present economic level.

From the Colonel

China is the epitome of the socialist state. It is a dictatorship wherein the central government is accountable to no one and is all-powerful. The Chinese leadership have long had the goal of becoming the dominant nation in the world. They now have the second largest economy in the world—behind the US—and they are growing their military and are quite advanced in internet and technology warfare. They do want to destroy us.

The citizens of Hong Kong are in a special category—they have some freedoms—at least for a while. Their citizens are protesting denouncing socialism and waiving the American flag—this while some of our students are protesting seeking socialism.

We must be sure that our citizens and students study China and its influence in and on the world. We must understand both what a real socialist state is and how great are both their ambitions and their resources.

– Denny Gillem

Declaration of Independence, para 2

*We the People of the United States,
in Order to form a more perfect
Union, establish Justice, insure
domestic Tranquility, provide for
the common defence, promote the
general Welfare, and secure the
Blessings of Liberty to ourselves
and our Posterity, do ordain and
establish this Constitution for the
United States of America.*

Preamble to US Constitution

CHAPTER 8

POLITICIANS, DON'T INSULT US BY ASSUMING WE DON'T KNOW OUR RIGHTS GIVEN BY THE CONSTITUTION

BY MARC LIEBMAN

I T'S ELECTION SEASON, AGAIN! Politicians are again demonstrating an amazing lack of knowledge about the Constitution and the rights and protections it provides to the citizens of the United States of America.

It is even more amazing that many candidates who are or were elected officials have forgotten the words in the document that gave them the power of their office. Each of them swore the oath of office in Article II, Section 1, paragraph 8 that they must take before assuming office. While specifically referencing the president, the oath in the Constitution sets the standard for the oath taken by every member of the House of Representatives, the Senate, Federal Judges and members of the military. It is as follows:

> *"I do solemnly swear (or affirm) that I will faithfully execute the Office of President of the United States, and will to the best of my Ability, preserve, protect and defend the Constitution of the United States."*

When an elected member of the Federal government speaks, he or she should be mindful of the contents of the document he or she has sworn to uphold, and he or she should understand the powers and limitations of power defined in the Constitution. If you haven't read it recently, here's a link – https://constitutionus.com. It will take you thirty minutes to read and even longer to contemplate the wisdom of its contents.

After reading the Constitution – the document on which the greatest democracy ever created was built – use it as a framework to help evaluate a candidate's statements. What follows are four candidate statements that have come in 2019.

American Military Veterans

"I'll make it illegal to join the NRA
(and other organizations) ..."

During a Democratic debate, one candidate was cheered when the individual stated, "If I am elected president, I will make membership in NRA (and other organizations) illegal...."

According to the polling firm Rasmussen, 28 percent of Democrats believe membership in the NRA should be illegal. The NRA has been vilified by the left, even though they have no idea what the NRA does or how it operates other than it is a pro-legal gun ownership organization. The NRA is not alone; it just gets the most attention from the left.

Whether you like the NRA or not, is not relevant. What is relevant is any attempt to make it illegal to join the NRA (or any organization that has not advocated violence or conducted subversive or seditious activity) because it violates the Constitution.

The First Amendment of the Constitution states:

> *"Congress shall make no law*
> *respecting an establishment of*
> *religion or prohibiting the free*
> *exercise thereof; or abridging the*
> *freedom of speech or the press;*
> *or the right of people peaceably*
> *to assemble and to petition*

the Government to redress of grievances."

If these words don't make it clear that passing a law to prohibit membership in an organization that has committed no crime other than opposing your point of view, then read it again.

"We're going to take your AR-15s, your AK-47s...."

In mid-September 2019, a presidential candidate went on an emotional rant after the horrendous mass shooting in an El Paso WalMart saying, assuming he was elected president:

"Hell yes, we're going to take your AR-15s, your AK-47s .... We're going to take all your guns away..."

If he, as president were to act on this pledge, his administration would violate three articles of the Constitution. Which side of the gun debate you are on, is again, irrelevant.

Let's start with the most obvious violation.

1.   The right to keep and bear arms

Article II of the Bill of Rights states:

"A well-regulated militia being necessary to the security of a free state the right of the people to keep and bear arms shall not be infringed.

So, until the Supreme Court declares the Second Amendment unconstitutional, or the country goes through the process to repeal the Second Amendment as defined in the Constitution, it is the law of the land.

2.   Illegal search and seizure

Next, on what basis would this candidate order law enforcement agencies around the country to go house to house and seize weapons? Article IV of the Bill of Rights (the first ten amendments to the Constitution) states:

> *"The right of the people to be secure in their persons, houses, papers and effects against unreasonable searches and seizures shall not be violated. No warrants shall issue, but upon probable cause supported by oath or affirmation and particularly describing the place to be searched, the persons or things to be searched."*

If an American citizen legally owns a firearm and has not committed, nor there is evidence he or she is about to commit a crime with it, there is no probable cause or legal basis for a search. In other words, the search is illegal.

3.   The right to due process

The candidate's proposal also runs afoul of Article V of the Bill of Rights. It guarantees us the right to due process by stating:

> *"No person shall be held to answer for a capital or otherwise infamous crime unless on a presentment or indictment of a grand jury, except in cases arising in the land or naval forces, or in the militia, when in actual service in time of war or public danger; nor shall any person be subject for the same offense to be twice put in jeopardy of life or limb; nor shall be compelled in any criminal case to be a witness against himself, nor be deprived of life, liberty, or property without due process of law; nor shall private property be taken for public use without just compensation."*

Proponents of seizing an individual's firearms have two questions to answer. One ... where's the crime? Without evidence of probable cause, prosecutors cannot go to a judge for a search or an arrest warrant. Two ... if you are a gun owner and your historic firearms are seized, who determines the just compensation and what's the process?

American Military Veterans

*"If elected, I would abolish the
Electoral College ..."*

The Electoral College is established in Article II, Section I, Item 3 and is further clarified in the Twelfth Amendment.

A little history is in order here. The Founding Fathers didn't want the big, more populous states to dominate the smaller ones any more than they do today. In other words, if you live in Kansas or North Dakota, do you want representatives from New York and California dictating national policy?

If you need an example, look at California. The extremely liberal counties around San Francisco, Los Angeles and Sacramento dictate state policy, often to the detriment of those who live in less populated counties.

This is the reasoning why, when writing the Constitution, the Founding Fathers stipulated two houses in Congress. One, the Senate, where every state has two Senators and, two, the House, which is based on population. The total of Senators plus representatives dictates how many electoral votes a state has.

Imperfect as it is, the Electoral College works. The Democrats would want you to believe that Trump's election was the first time a candidate won the popular vote and lost the electoral one. It isn't. It has happened five times in U.S. history.

1. Andrew Jackson won the popular vote but lost in the Electoral College to John Quincy Adams in 1824 when several electors refused to vote for Jackson and the House of Representatives – as per the Constitution - decided in favor of Jackson.

2. In 1876, Samuel Tilden won 3.05% more votes than Rutherford B. Hayes and lost by one electoral vote.

3. Twelve years later, in 1888 Grover Cleveland received .82% more votes than Benjamin Harrison who earned 16.21% more electoral votes (233 to 168).

4. Al Gore won the popular vote by .53% but lost by five electoral votes (.93%) in 2000.

5. Sixteen years later, Hillary Clinton earned 2.21% more popular votes than Donald Trump but lost the election by 77 (304 – 277) electoral votes or 14.5%.

The Electoral College system works as our Founding Fathers intended. This means you can lose the Presidency even if you win big in the popular vote in New York, California and Illinois, but not do well in the rest of the country, just as our Founding Fathers intended.

SO YOU WANT TO CHANGE THE CONSTITUTION?

Since several candidates have mentioned they want to toss out the Electoral College and repeal the Second Amendment, here's the process defined in the Constitution in Article V:

> *The Congress, whenever two thirds of both houses shall deem it necessary, shall propose amendments to this Constitution, or, on the application of the legislatures of two thirds of the several states, shall call a convention for proposing amendments, which, in either case, shall be valid to all intents and purposes, as part of this Constitution, when ratified by the legislatures of three fourths of the several states, or by conventions in three fourths thereof, as the one or the other mode of ratification may be proposed by the Congress; provided that no amendment which may be made prior to the year one thousand eight hundred and eight shall in any manner affect the first and fourth clauses in the ninth section of the first article; and that no state, without its consent, shall*

be deprived of its equal suffrage in the Senate.

Translation.

1. Either both houses of the Congress can begin the process by approving a potential amendment by a two-thirds majority or two-thirds of the state legislatures (33 of 50) can propose one.

2. Then, two-thirds of the state legislatures must hold Constitutional Amendment sessions and three-quarters of all the state legislatures (38 of 50) must approve the amendment which then goes back to Congress.

3. The house must ratify the proposed amendment by a two thirds vote of its members.

Yes, our Founding Fathers deliberately made it hard and time consuming to avoid disasters like the 18th Amendment which banned the sale of alcohol and was a windfall for organized crime. It took 14 years before it was repealed by the 21st Amendment and is the only Constitutional Amendment that has been repealed.

Since our Constitution was ratified in 1789, it has been amended only 27 times. The first 10 (the Bill of Rights) came as part of an agreement to get the Massachusetts legislature to ratify the Constitution. The Bill of Rights was approved by Congress within two years after the ratification of the Constitution.

When Louis XVI, the King of France, threw his weight behind the American rebels in March 1778 and declared war on England, it was not because he believed in our cause. France was still smarting from a recent defeat by the British in the Seven Years War that ended in 1765. Louis XVI wanted revenge for the results of a war that cost France all of Canada, amongst other possessions. Our part of the Seven Years War is known as the French and Indian War.

In 1789, the French Revolution was, in many ways, inspired by our own American Revolution. Louis XVI was beheaded in 1793, and the first French Constitution was ratified in 1791. Since then, the French hold the record among democracies by having voted upon and accepted 16 different constitutions. One was in effect for only 21 days.

IN CONCLUSION

The United States has been blessed because our Founding Fathers wrote one of the most brilliant documents of its kind in history. Our Constitution has been in force for 230+ years and is the oldest document of its kind that is still in force today. Let's continue to expand on this record.

Marc Liebman is a retired Navy Captain and Naval Aviator who served during Vietnam, Desert Shield/Storm. He is an award winning author of six novels who views himself has a hard line independent who believes in term limits for ALL elected officials.

From the Founders

If you don't know what our founding documents say, then our nation is at risk because no one is keeping us on track. Please make sure your family is very familiar with these documents.

"We hold these truths to be self-evident, that all men are created equal, that they are endowed by their Creator with certain unalienable Rights, that among these are Life, Liberty and the pursuit of Happiness. — That to secure these rights, Governments are instituted among Men, deriving their just powers from the consent of the governed, — That whenever any Form of Government becomes destructive of these ends, it is the Right of the People to alter or to abolish it, and to institute new Government, laying its foundation on such principles and organizing its powers in such form, as to them shall seem most likely to effect their Safety and Happiness."

Historical Perspective

Our nation has two founding documents, the Declaration of Independence and the Constitution. Most American citizens know of these documents but have never read them—and our nation is much the worse for this. A great many Americans do celebrate the 4th of July—but don't know why they celebrate it—beyond knowing it's "Independence Day." Well, on 4 July 1776 the Continental Congress passed the Declaration of Independence. One of the things that document states is that our rights come—not from the government—but from God. The declaration declared war on England and formally began our Revolutionary War. The Congress also passed the Articles of Confederation which loosely tied the states together so we could fight for our freedom.

After the war the Congress met to revise the Articles of Confederation. They ended up starting from scratch—and our Constitution was the result. We all do need to know what it says and to hold all government officials to its standards. To help our nation move away from influence by the swamp, we all must know what this document says and hold all elected officials accountable.

There will be boots on the ground if there's to be any hope of success in the strategy.

– Robert M Gates

This pair of boots was found by the photography at the Vietnam Memorial Wall. There was a note inside from a loved one to the previous owner of the boots. It's important to remember that all who go into battle for freedom's cause may fall. That is the ultimate price of freedom.

And that is why ...
we honor and remember.

STEPHAN L BECHTE
LBERTO CACERES • DONALD R COL
NALD A HAUSRATH Jr • PETER A HILL
NIS M KEEFE
ALD J KELLEY • C
HAEL J MU
CHARLES E McDO
PH H REID
HART • R
HARD L SO
ORGE E TA

"Loyalty to country ALWAYS. Loyalty to government, when it deserves it."

– Mark Twain

"They wrote in the old days that it is sweet and fitting to die for one's country. But in modern war, there is nothing sweet nor fitting in your dying. You will die like a dog for no good reason."

– Ernest Hemingway

CHAPTER 9

"THE DANGEROUS EVOLUTION OF FALSE PATRIOTISM"

BY CHIPP NAYLON

TO BEGIN, I MUST EMPHAsize that this is an opinion piece, nothing more than me standing up on a soapbox and giving voice to my frustrations. And, as an American, a Marine Corps combat veteran, and a generally cynical human being, I feel an obligation to vent these frustrations – not to impose my views, but to at least give them a voice. As such, please do not confuse this for an academic article or official document. Rather, I simply hope to explore the evolution of false patriotism that has taken root in post-9/11 America, a phenomenon I view as an existential threat to our way of life.

On September 11th, 2001, our country came under attack. For a moment, the fractiousness of US politics and culture clash fell to the way-side as we united under common cause – righteous indignation and a fierce desire for justice. Over the burning embers of the World Trade Center, Pentagon, and fields of Somerset County, Pennsylvania, Americans responded as one, overcoming our differences to pursue a common enemy.

In this common pursuit of justice, less than a month after the September 11th attacks, US forces invaded Afghanistan. The objective: destroy the al Qaeda operatives who planned these attacks and their Taliban hosts.

Merriam-Webster defines patriotism as:

"love for or devotion to one's country."

While I am inherently skeptical of absolutes, during this time in US history, one would be hard-pressed to find an American not brimming with this patriotism, that is, a true love of our country and the way of life it represents. We had been attacked, and our love of country necessitated a just response. In this context, military action was an inevitable and logical extension of patriotism, as defending America and defeating its enemies in Afghanistan became indivisible objectives.

This unity underpinning America's post-9/11 patriotism proved short-lived. As US policy makers shifted focus to Saddam Hussein's Iraq, putting Afghanistan and the true pursuit of justice in the rearview, the brief reprieve from contentious political divisions shattered. Regardless of concerns – justified or not – of weapons of mass destruction in Iraq, Saddam Hussein had not attacked the United States on September 11th. Consequently, as US politicians sought to mobilize support for the invasion of Iraq, military action no longer remained inextricably linked with the September 11th attacks. No longer could our elected officials look us in the eyes and say, "We are pursuing those responsible for attacking our homeland, and this pursuit justifies the use of military force." In place of this clear connection, a tenuous logic arose somehow tying the invasion of Iraq to the defense of our homeland.

This tenuous logic brought inevitable questions – and pushback – from people who saw through its shaky foundation. People rightly began to ask that question dreaded by all people seeking to suppress logic – "Why?" Specifically, why are we invading Iraq? And, more pointedly, why are we committing to this military action when we have failed to hold those actually responsible for the September 11th attacks accountable? As these questions could not be answered with logic, US policy makers bent on the invasion of Iraq turned to a more nefarious method to generate support: establishing the false dichotomy of with-us-or-against-us. In other words, if you don't support the invasion of Iraq, you must not support America. Remember "freedom fries?" Despite serving as a steadfast ally in our pursuit of justice in Afghanistan, France had the audacity to question the rationale for invading Iraq, refusing to provide troops in the process. Embracing the above false dichotomy, US policy makers argued that, in failing to support our invasion of Iraq, France no longer supported the United States as a whole.

Domestically, this false dichotomy manifested itself in a far more dangerous way than trite name changes a la "freedom" fries. In US culture, this with-us-or-against-us argument evolved into a perverted version of the patriotism – that love of America – that united our country in the dark days following September 11th. Embracing this flawed logic, the phenomenon of false patriotism arose, the idea that, "if you love America, you must blindly support its use of military force." Do you have the audacity to question our military misadventures overseas? You must be against freedom, as well.

In the hands of US officials bent on continued military operations overseas, this false patriotism has been a potent weapon. When people question the rationale behind our seemingly endless wars, they face a common response: "We are defending our way of life, and a failure to support these combat operations must mean that you oppose this way of life." This is a patently absurd conclusion, but clearly it remains effective. Eighteen years after Congress's Authorization for Use of Military Force (AUMF) provided the legal justification to pursue the September 11th perpetrators, this document remains a blank check for any and all combat operations remotely related to Islamic extremism.

Hiding behind the flawed logic of false patriotism, Congress has abdicated its military oversight responsibilities, effectively granting the executive branch free reign in the conduct of military operations. While it may be political suicide to acknowledge, terrorism is not an existential threat to the United States. On September 11th, al Qaeda operatives succeeded in the most horrific terror attack in United States history. Yet, despite the horrors of this attack, we emerged stronger as a nation, united in love of country and the way of life America represents. In no way, shape, or form did these terrorists represent a risk to the end of this great experiment in democracy.

However, in the years following September 11th, our response to terrorism has created an existential threat to the United States. By allowing the AUMF to remain in force, Congress has shaken the foundation of the American system. Built on a system of checks and balances between the three branches of government, our Constitution grants Congress the power to declare war for a reason – an executive branch with unrestrained power to use our nation's military constitutes too significant a threat to democracy. As such, we currently find ourselves in a dangerous situation. Continued abdication of Congress's military oversight role all but guarantees a slide down the slippery slope towards unchecked executive branch power to conduct military operations. And, at risk of appearing hyperbolic, can a democracy continue to exist when no check to endless combat operations exists?

What, then, is the call to action for patriotic Americans? From a philosophical perspective, we must first shatter the flawed logic of false patriotism. To question the merits of American military operations does not mean one hates freedom. Quite the contrary, demanding honest and open debate about the merits (or lack thereof) of military force goes hand-in-hand with a love for the American men and women carrying out that force – and the country they serve. Next, we must hold our elected officials accountable, demanding that Congress fulfill its military oversight role. From a practical perspective, this means revoking the AUMF. This post-9/11 authorization can no longer serve as a blank check for combat operations. Prior to sending our men and women in uniform into harm's way, Congress must conduct its due diligence by: A) debating and defining the political objectives driving military force, and B) ensuring a logical link between that military force and its overarching political objectives exists. Endless combat operations for the sake of combat operations cannot remain the norm.

To reiterate the Merriam-Webster definition, patriotism entails "love for or devotion to one's country." Quotes from two pillars of American literature introduced this essay. Shattering the phenomenon of false patriotism means embracing Mark Twain's argument, because the unfortunate alternative is realizing Hemingway's. We owe our men and women in uniform more than this outcome.

Maurice "Chipp" Naylon is a former Marine Corps infantry officer, combat veteran, and the author of *The New Ministry of Truth: Combat Advisors in Afghanistan and America's Great Betrayal.*

From the Colonel

The last time Congress declared war was in December 1941, after Japan bombed Pearl Harbor, Hawaii. On 8 December Congress declared war on Japan. On 11 December Congress declared war on Japan's allies, Germany and Italy.

After the declaration of war our entire nation mobilized for war. There was already a draft—it stepped up. Many products, like food and clothes and gasoline, were rationed. Industry stopped producing consumer goods like automobiles—so all our industry could produce combat vehicles and aircraft. Individual families planted victory gardens around their homes so that they would need less food from other sources—so that farm products could be used to feed our troops and our allies. Bottom line, with the declaration of war the entire nation went to war—not just the military.

In Korea and Vietnam, Panama, the Gulf Wars, and the wars against terrorist organizations none of the above happened.

Let's honor our military by sending them into only wars that Congress has declared—and only into wars where the enemy is named and victory defined.

I do not mean that we should not send a military force into brief situations—like we should have in Benghazi. Nor do I mean that we should stop sending our special operations forces out to hunt terrorists.

–Denny Gillem

The World War II Memorial opened to the public on April 29, 2004. It honors the 16 million who served in the armed forces of our great country, over 400,000 who died, and all those who supported the war effort from home.

Amendment 1 - Ratified 12/15/1791.

Congress shall make no law respecting an establishment of religion, or prohibiting the free exercise thereof; or abridging the freedom of speech, or of the press; or the right of the people peaceably to assemble, and to petition the Government for a redress of grievances.

If the press (media) isn't free then it's controlled by the government and we have no chance of knowing what is really happening in our nation.

When something happens, the news-media has three options. 1. Report the facts—that's what the news is supposed to do. 2. Report some facts and add opinion—now it's not news; it's opinion. 3. Ignore it.

Almost no news media simply report the facts—as they did do when I was growing up. They either give facts and opinion (in this situation you can go online and find "the rest of the story" if you wish). Or they can ignore it—and you don't research it because you don't know about it.

CHAPTER 10

MAIN STREAM MEDIA PERVERSION

BY ROBERT H. ORR

ARE OUR MAINSTREAM media biased politically? Absolutely, if you are looking for a one-word answer. And for the sake of this chapter, we will restrict our discussion to the leading city and town newspapers and the television media consisting of both local news outlets and major news networks such as Fox News, MSNBC and CNN. We will look briefly at the potential difficulties caused by social media outlets like Facebook along with the world wide web and their potential to influence those seeking the truth in the news.

There are many schools of journalism located throughout the United States. Assuredly, most, if not all, stress the importance of journalistic ethics. Ethics can be both an elusive as well as a subjective term. It concerns itself with the moral philosophy of what is right and what is wrong; what is good or what is evil. And therein lies our dilemma. Not everyone takes their moral direction from the same source. Ethical journalism involves truth in reporting and avoiding journalism bias. This latter term is defined as avoiding the intentional misleading of the readership, listenership or viewership by slanting presentations in such a way as to lead the recipients to incomplete or wrong conclusions. So, how then, do certain media institutions "lean left" or "lean right?" Is there bias in journalism after all? The short answer is yes, of course.

Some journalistic bias is unintentional and unavoidable. Here is one major reason why. Psychologically, we all view the world differently. I have worked for people and taught people who cannot wrap their minds around the phrase "exception to policy." To them, this phrase is an oxymoron. If you have a policy, there can be no exceptions; otherwise it is not a policy. In the military, the phrase was often invoked to receive temporary dispensation from a policy or regulation that simply did not fit a particular set of circumstances. Those who would authorize exceptions viewed the notion that a policy was a guideline, but not an absolute proclamation. Why the difference in attitude?

One strong possibility lies in the theory of personality types first introduced in the 1920s by Carl Jung. Two decades later, Isabel Briggs Myers and her mother, so fascinated with Jung's ideas, developed through their own research, a method that assessed personality type along four axes: introversion/extroversion, intuition/sensation, thinking/feeling and perception/judgment. The resulting testing instrument produced sixteen different types of personality indicators. Each is different in one or more aspects from the others, but all collectively help define who we think we are, how we learn, what we prefer, how we assess the world around us and so forth. There is ample information available on the Myers Briggs Type Indicator (MBTI) online to satisfy the most inquisitive of us. So let's return to our journalist.

The journalist writes an article about a topic of interest to you as a reader. Despite every conscious attempt to remain impartial and unbiased, the journalist has a psychological makeup that helps determine how he or she views the world. Add to the mix, parental, spiritual and intellectual influences and we wind up with a presentation of facts in a way that marries to the journalist's view of the world. If the reader has a similar set of influences and personality type, the two resonate. Truth, as written by the journalist and absorbed by the reader is congruent. But what if the reader's personality type and/or set of influences differs radically from the journalist? "Lies" or "fake news," screams the reader. So, was the journalist truthful or deceiving? This is one major dilemma we face today in ascertaining whether the media is perverting truth.

Another problem in dealing with media presentations is typified in the following example. I read a headline and byline to a newspaper column. I am intrigued. I read the article and then am left scratching my head. The headline and byline preconditioned me. I was expecting something and got something else. How did this happen? Perhaps an editor chose the headings to attract readers. In today's electronic world, managers keep track of likes, retweets, forwards, number of accesses and so forth. Not only do those managers learn which columnists are being read the most, they also begin to find out current interests of the readership. The newspaper is, after all, in the business of making money. So are radio and television media. There will be a tendency to cater to that readership. This catering leads to a slightly intentional bias, as in keep the customers happy.

In the video arena, keeping the customers happy is compounded by a need to keep the (advertising) sponsors happy. Based on 2017 data, a 30-second spot on the cable news networks cost anywhere from $2500 – $9,000. The revenues from advertising alone could approach $250,000 per hour per network. Sponsors need viewers, else they will spend their marketing dollars elsewhere. To attract viewers, these networks may need to hire the so-called "rock stars" of the news world. Egos may be involved as well as content control issues. And of course, there is the daily need to contract for topic experts to keep the news shows interesting and entertaining. Some shows have an inherent bias; some commentators and moderators attempt to present both sides of an issue. In the end, the viewers are left with the burden of deciding what is factual, what is opinion and what is pure fantasy – certainly a daunting task.

Life would be much simpler if each news show would just hand us the truth, the whole truth, and nothing but the truth. Now that is a fantasy! Instead, the burden is on the readers, listeners and viewers to read carefully and intelligently, listen critically, view with attentiveness, avoid prejudging, and above all, to think critically to evaluate better and sift through the noise to get at the truth. That process is hard work. But it is our burden and if we shun it, we risk putting the fate of our republic in the hands of those who seek and hold power.

I have avoided categorizing social media, podcasts and other forums supported by the world wide web within the umbrella of mainstream media. But events in our recent history suggest that this outlet for real news, fake news, opinion and disinformation dissemination is a force to be reckoned with. Regulation of this outlet is not strong; indeed, constitutionally protected free speech underlies how outlets such as Facebook might be utilized. Owners of these outlets are reluctant to exercise censorship beyond very limited bounds. A recent event involving Facebook demonstrates an issue of monumental future concern; namely, what exactly constitutes fake news and who gets to make that determination?

A small group of senators intervened recently when Facebook decided to fact check some dubious claims published on Facebook by an anti-abortion group. The fact-checkers published a finding that some of the group's claims were false. At this point the U. S. senators intervened and pressured the owner of Facebook to remove the fact-check claims, which sadly, he did. Congressional intervention in internet-based published information sets a dangerous precedent. This incident is a brief synopsis of an article recently written by Chris Sikich of the Indianapolis Star and the USA

TODAY NETWORK.

Nearly forty-five years ago, I was teaching short courses for government executives and administrators regarding the emerging field of management information systems. When discussing a perceived dilemma that executives lacked sufficient relevant information upon which to base their decisions, we were fond of responding that "today's managers suffer from an overabundance of irrelevant information wherein lay the relevant information." This was at a time when the world wide web was essentially a research exchange conduit among leading universities that were able to use the network whose primary purpose was to support our government's World Wide Military Command and Control System. How times have changed. Now the average citizen is bombarded with an overabundance of information from too many sources. To sift through this morass is overwhelming. Yet as responsible citizens, it is our responsibility to validate our sources and to systematically search for the truth as it relates to whatever issue is of concern to us at the moment. Noise filters? As many as you can find. Keep seeking for truth; for truth is elusive and often in need of refinement as we uncover more relevant information.

Robert Orr was born and raised in Philadelphia, Pennsylvania. He graduated from West Point in 1964 with a BS degree in General Engineering, served in a variety of command, staff and teaching positions during his 21 years of military service, which included a tour in Vietnam with the 4th Infantry Division. Upon retiring from military service in 1985, he took a teaching position at Indiana University Purdue University Indianapolis (IUPUI) in the field of computer and information technology. During his 21 years of university service, he specialized in business data communications, quantitative reasoning and writing across the curriculum. From 2001-2006, also served as Director of Indiana University's Teaching Academy. He retired in 2006 with the rank of Professor emeritus. Since that time, he has served as a volunteer track and field coach for Westfield (IN) High School specializing in sprints and vertical jumps. He currently resides in Westfield, Indiana.

What You Can Do

Unfortunately, today the Main-Stream Media seems to be in lock-step with the radical-left wing of the Democratic Party. Fox News seems to be the only media that even occasionally mentions good things that Republicans have done or wrong things that Democrats have done. Thus, watching the news is brainwashing—not education.

Regardless of where an individual stands politically, we all need to get "just the facts." Then we can listen to commentators or do other research, if we wish.

We Americans must find and support "fact-focused" media, and avoid any support of today's biased media.

''*Success is not final, failure is not fatal: it is the courage to continue that counts.*''

— Winston Churchill, Prime Minister of England during World War II

CHAPTER 11

SUICIDE

BY JIM PIDGEON

VETERAN AND ACTIVE duty military suicide is a complex and multifaceted issue. There is no shortage of opinions, myths, studies, reports and reasons. We can trace its roots all the way back to the Revolutionary War.

U.S. CIVIL WAR

The Union Army reported 391 official suicides during the Civil War. There was no official report on Confederate side. Thomas Evans of the 12th U.S. Regulars, reported after the battle of Mayre's

Heights, finding a dead soldier with a rifle laying parallel on top of his body, with powder burns
on his uniform and his "head shattered from the
chin up." The soldiers feared the brutal and horrific battlefield medical treatment. Stories of the
screams and the piles of severed arms and legs,
battlefield amputations and lakes of blood. It was
also reported of the soldier's fear, on both sides,
of being captured by the enemy and placed in
makeshift wire fence POW camps, in some cases
"ear shot" from the battlefield. Torture, humilia-
tion and starvation were common in the camps.
One POW, Francis Amasa Walker, wrote of his
experience as a POW.

> *"A period of nervous horror such
> as I had never before and have
> never since experienced and
> memories of which have always
> made it perfectly clear how one can
> be driven on, unwillingly and vainly
> resisting, to commit suicide."*

Crossing these wire fences, termed "the dead
line" was another form of suicide. It was reported
one soldier crossed the line and challenged the
sentry to shoot him. After two missed shots, the
POW yelled at the sentry "to do his duty." The
third shot was a head shot that killed him instantly.

American Military Veterans

WORLD WAR I

Fast forward fifty-four years to WWI. Combatant governments on both sides of the Atlantic, struggled with how to deal with military suicide, war trauma and mental illness. An American psychiatrist, Dr. Thomas Salmon, reported 400 American veterans died by suicide in New York State alone. Unfortunately, the American returning veterans mental health was basically left to personal responsibility. "Shell shock" was widely reported, filmed and documented. Many severely wounded with horrible facial injuries and loss of limbs. Films and pictures were plentiful of the masks for the facial wounds and the early prosthetic limb technology. Veterans returned to work on the farms and in the factories. Less than a decade later, the stock market crashed. Many lost their jobs and homes. Unemployment, homelessness, soup kitchens and food lines would follow. Veteran health care was blown away in the "Dust Bowl of the Great Depression."

WORLD WAR II

A few years later, WWII, the attack on Pearl Harbor, December 7, 1941. "A Date which will live in Infamy" in President Franklin D. Roosevelt's historic address to Congress, asking a State of

War be declared between the United States and Japan. In 1944, The Servicemen's Readjustment Act was passed to accommodate the soon to be returning veterans. The Act was a huge step to assist American veterans, but far from perfect. The Cold War would follow.

THE KOREAN CONFLICT

June 25, 1950, 75,000 North Korean troops poured across the 38th Parallel. The Korean War had begun. The Servicemen's Act of WWll was only six years old, but was still in it's infancy and mostly ineffective. I found no reliable suicide numbers during the Korean Conflict in which 5.7 million U.S. troops served, and 54,246 total U.S. deaths and 36,574 died in the theater. American officials considered the war against the forces of International Communism itself, and the fear of WWlll, possibly facing the Soviet Union and China as real. Five million soldiers and civilians lost their lives in the Korean Conflict. In July of 1953 the hostilities ceased. U.S. troops are still on guard South of the 38th Parallel today.

THE VIETNAM WAR

November 22, 1963 President John F. Kennedy was assassinated in Dallas Texas. The whole nation was in shock. Lyndon B. Johnson was sworn in as

President. Then, on August 2nd and 4th 1964, two unprovoked attacks by North Vietnamese torpedo boats on two USN destroyers, the Maddox and the Turner Joy occurred. The attacks led to The Gulf of Tonkin Resolution, which allowed President Johnson to escalate U.S. Military involvement in the Vietnam War. On March 5, 1965 the U.S. First Marines landed in DaNang. During the Vietnam War 27,709,918 Americans served in uniform. Unconfirmed reports estimated 50,000 or more Vietnam veterans committed suicide. Military morality studies suggest the best estimate is that 9,000 committed suicide. 58,148 were killed in Vietnam.

GULF WAR OPERATION DESERT SHIELD.

Desert Shield occurred from August 2, 1990 to Feb. 28, 1991. U.S. total casualties sustained were 372. Of these, 147 were combat related, and 194 were non battlefield injuries. 30 died by illness. My research found no military suicide report.

AFGHANISTAN AND IRAQ WARS

The war in Afghanistan occurred from October 1, 2001 to October 2018. The Iraq War from March, 2003 to October 2018. Total casualties, Afghanistan 2,401. Iraq 6951. Suicide was reported as an urgent and growing problem. In both

Wars combined, there were more than 6,000 total suicides each year from 2008-2016, a rate that is 1.5 times greater than that of the non-veteran population. The *Guardian* reported in September 2018, that young military veterans suicide rates had jumped substantially. Many of the veterans in these reports served in the Afghanistan and Iraq Wars. AMVETS National Executive Director Joe Chenelly and Marine Combat Veteran commented as follows:

> *"This isn't just alarming, it's a*
> *National Emergency that requires*
> *immediate action. We've spent*
> *the last decade trying to improve*
> *the transitioning process for our*
> *veterans, but we're clearly failing*
> *and people are dying."*

WOMAN VETERAN SUICIDE

According to the VA Report dated April 2019, women are the fastest growing veteran population, totaling 9% of the entire U.S. military veteran population. Women veteran suicide counts and rates have decreased from 2015-2016. Women veterans are more likely to die by suicide than non-veteran women. Women veterans are more likely than non-veteran women to use a firearm as a method of suicide.

American Military Veterans

SUICIDE FACTS

In 2013, the VA released a study that covered suicides from 1999-2010, showing that approximately 22 veterans died by suicide everyday, or one every 65 minutes. In 2012, for the first time, more active duty service members died by suicide than died in combat. A February 4, 2016 study reported that non combat veterans are more likely to commit suicide than combat veterans. The Department of Veterans Affairs or VA, says in its National Suicide Data Report, that young veteran suicide deaths have increased, as the overall veteran suicide rates has decreased. More than 70% of veterans who have died by suicide have not recently received health care service from the VA.

SUICIDE CAUSES

Post Traumatic Stress Disorder, PTSD. A study by the VA found that veterans are more likely to develop symptoms of PTSD for many reasons such as longer times at war, lower education level, more severe combat conditions, other soldiers around them, brain/head trauma, female gender, life-lasting physical injuries and military structure.

Numerous Non Profit Organizations, spread all across the nation, have reported to help veterans with PTSD, TBI, depression, nightmares and social anxiety. The use of service dogs and equine horses have many documented success reports. Guitar music therapy, camping, hunting and fishing programs are other alternative treatments that have shown promise helping veterans.

FEDERAL POLICY INITIATIVES/LAWS.

One important law in 2007 was the Joshua Omvig Veterans Suicide Prevention Act. This act created a comprehensive program to reduce veteran suicide. Named for a veteran who committed suicide in 2005. The law directed the Secretary of the U.S. Department of Veteran Affairs to implement a comprehensive suicide prevention program. The program was to include stall education, mental health assessments as a part of overall health assessments, a suicide prevention coordinator at every VA medical facility, research efforts, 24-hour mental health care, a toll free crisis line and outreach to educate veterans and their families. In 2009, the VA added a one-to-one "chat service" for veterans who prefer to reach out for help on the Internet. In 2010, the National Action Alliance for Suicide Prevention was created. In 2012, the National Strategy was revised with the Obama Administration Suicide Prevention Strategies for Veterans. A goal was formed to make the process of finding and obtaining mental health resources easier for veterans, to work to recruit and retain mental health professionals and make the government programs more accountable to the veterans they serve.

ADDITIONAL VA SUICIDE RATE REPORT HIGHLIGHTS

The findings show there is a variability across the country in rates and numbers of veteran suicides. Overall the numbers mirror those of the same population and geographic region with the highest rates in the Western states, although we see higher rates of suicide in some smaller populations. Veteran suicides are still heaviest in populated areas. The rate among middle age and older veterans remains high. In 2014 almost 65 percent of all veterans were 50 years of age or above. After adjusting for differences in age and sex the risk of suicide was 22% higher among veterans when compared to non-veteran adults. After adjusting for differences in age, the risk for suicide was 19% higher among males to U.S. non-veterans. After adjusting for differences in age the risk of suicide was 2.5 times higher among female veterans when compared to U.S. non-veteran adult women.

THE UPDATED-9, 2018 OMHSP NATIONAL SUICIDE DATA REPORT 2005-2006

Data compiled for the research study started in 2005 and ended in 2014. After two years of compiling, the report came out in 2016. Despite grave numbers, the suicide rate among veterans is still only 1.5 times higher that the national average of non-veterans. The crisis has gained prominence because veteran and funeral benefits don't reflect their service and/or the family sacrifice. In addition the reports big news is this: the biggest group of soldier suicide comes from older veterans, aged 50 and above, mostly living in the western part of the country and are more likely to commit suicide due to PTSD and poor VA local inadequate mental health services.

VETERANS LOST TO TRAUMA AND NOT COMBAT

Sometimes trauma can be more deadly than war itself with VA existing mental health services that are woefully inadequate for a growing problem.

Veterans should not be dying in a VA parking lot. Existing mental health services are clearly insufficient. From 2001 to 2014, these veteran suicides have jumped to 32 percent, and the problem is only going to get worse. A 76-year-old veteran shot himself in the parking lot of his Long Island VA facility, because "he went to the ER and was denied service." But improving treatment requires more resources. Our mental health system must also evolve its therapeutic paradigms to be more proactive, treating the root causes of mental illness. Too often, VA facilities are purely reactive, only kicking into action once the veteran is suffering a crisis. Proactively addressing the precursors to Suicidal Ideation can prevent the crisis in the first place. It was reported by the Pentagon that there were 325 active duty military suicides from 2001-2008. Of these, the National Guard and Reserve members who were never federally activated, did not receive VA services. Within that group there were 919 suicides in 2017. In August 2019, the Air Force ordered all units to stand down to address rising suicide rates. As of the end of July the service had seen 78 suicides. In September 2019, three Navy sailors aboard the aircraft carrier USS George H.W. Bush, died in apparent suicides.

SUICIDE AND SUICIDAL THOUGHTS.

Your doctor may do a physical exam, tests and in-depth questioning about your mental and physical health to help determine what may be causing your suicidal thinking and to determine the best treatment. Most cases of suicidal thoughts are linked to an underlying mental health issue that can be treated. If this is the case, you may need to see a doctor who specializes in diagnosing and treating mental illness (psychiatrist) or other mental health provider.

PHYSICAL HEALTH CONDITIONS

In some cases, suicidal thinking may be linked to an underlying physical health problem. You may need blood tests and other tests to determine whether this is the case.

ALCOHOL AND DRUG MISUSE.

For many, alcohol or drugs play a role in suicidal thinking and completed suicide. Your doctor will want you to know whether you have any problems with alcohol or drug use. Such as bingeing or being unable to cut back or quit on your own. Many people who feel suicidal need treatment to help them stop, to reduce their suicidal thoughts.

MORAL INJURY IS THE WAR INSIDE

Sometimes trauma is deadlier than war: Some survive combat and attempt suicide at home. Many veterans are not so lucky. Moral injury was identified by Jonathan Shea in his 1994 book *Achilles in Vietnam*. Moral injury has also been researched by Veterans Affairs clinicians. Moral injury is the result of violating core moral foundations by causing or witnessing serious harm or failing to save others. Moral injury can feel like a war inside, because people's consciences cannot make sense of experiences that derailed their identities. Among the most challenging of moral injuries is being betrayed by people we trust and who violate what we believe is right.

Anyone can have a moral injury. It is not a mental health disorder, yet the suffering is intense. Those afflicted can be crushed by the guilt, tortured by the anxiety, trapped by emotional solitary confinement, immobilized by meaningless, haunted by the dead, frayed but over worked, seduced by drugs, gambling, or sex, consumed by outrage. Often, they can experience "all the above".

HOW TO PROCESS THE PAIN

Volunteers of America (VOA) has a week-long program, peer-facilitated moral injury program called Resilience Strength Training (RST). Many of the veterans who have gone through the program note that what they shared with their peers is something they would never have "told their therapists."

Medications. In some people, certain prescription or over the counter drugs can cause suicidal thinking.

Spravato Johnson & Johnson's Nasal Spray. The U.S. Food and Drug Administration approved the ketamine-derived nasal spray Spravato for treatment-resistant depression. It is aimed at people with depression who have tried two antidepressant drugs and have not improved. "We have not had a breakthrough treatment, a truly different treatment for depression in a long time," says Michael Thase, Professor of Psychiatric and Director of the Mood and Anxiety Disorders Treatment and Research Program in the Perelman School of Medicine at the University of Pennsylvania.

Treatment. Treatment of suicidal thoughts and behavior depends on your specific situation, including your level of suicide risk and what underlying problems may be causing your suicidal thoughts and behavior.

Emergencies. If you have attempted suicide and you are injured, call 911 or your local emergency number. Have someone else call if you are not alone. If you are not injured, but you're at immediate risk of harming yourself, call 911 or your local emergency number or call a suicide hotline number like 1-800-273-8255 and press 1.

Supporting a loved one who is chronically suicidal can be stressful and exhausting. You may be afraid and feel guilty and helpless. Take advantage of resources about suicide prevention and awareness. Also take care of yourself by getting support from family, friends and veteran service organizations like the Disabled American Veterans DAV, (dav.org), Veterans of Foreign Wars VFW (vfw.org), AMVETS. (amvets.org), American Legion (members.legion.org.) All these organizations have suicide awareness and prevention programs. Also several suicide prevention organizations like 22EVERYDAY in 2012 and 22KILL in 2015 through multiple 22 push up challenges everyday campaigns on the social media.

Prevention Hotline. In 2011, the Hotline was renamed the Veterans Crisis Line VCL. The goal was to provide 24/7, world class suicide prevention and crisis intervention services to Veterans, Service Members and their families. It must meet the demands by responding to over 500,000 calls per year, along with thousands of electronic chats and text messages and to initiate a rescue when indicated. It must also train staff to respond to Veterans and their families individual encounters during which a responder must make an assessment of the needs of the caller under stressful, time-sensitive conditions. Since its inception in 2007, the VCL has answered over three million calls and initiated the dispatch of emergency services to callers imminent crisis over 84,000 times. Since launching chat in 2009 and text services in November 2011, the VCL has answered nearly

359,000 and nearly 78,000 requests for chat and text services. In addition, the staff has forwarded more than 504,000 referrals to local VA Suicide Prevention Coordinators on behalf of Veterans to ensure continuity with the Veteran's local VA providers.

Supporting a loved one who is chronically suicidal can be stressful and exhausting. You may be afraid and feel guilty and helpless. Take advantage of resources about suicide prevention and awareness. There is no "cookie cutter, fits all answer."

CITATIONS..
1...popularmilitary.com Feb. 4, 2016
2...www.mayoclinic.org Sept. 6, 2019
3...onceasoldier.org
4...www.theguardian.com Sept. 26, 2018
5...www.va.gov   VA Suicide Prevention Efforts Jan. 3 2019
6...www.stripes.com   Nation Suicide Data Report 2005-2015
7...time.com   Veteran Suicide Crisis Simon Walker Sept. 6, 2019
8...www.militarytimes Sept. 26, 2018
9...wikipedia.org Causes PTSD 2017
10...www.uswings.com
11...www.ncbi.nlm.nil.gov June 1990
12...www.whitehouse.gov   Presidential Actions Mar. 5, 2019
13...www.usatoday.com   Opinion   Jan. 16,

2019

14...www.britannica.com   Gulf   of   Tonkin Incident 1964

15...http://koreajoongangdaily.joins.com   Apr. 6, 2018

16...www.forbes.com Spravato Mar. 5, 2019

17...wikipedia.org-PREVENTS   Initiative May 2019

18...www.publichealth.va.gov U.S. Dept. of Veterans Affairs

19...www.mayoclinic.org Suicide and Suicidal Thoughts

20...Watson Institute Brown University   Costs of War Nov. 2018

21...wikipedia.org   U.S.   Military   Veteran Suicide

22...www.va.gov   U.S. Dept. of Veterans Affairs   Women Veterans   Apr. 2019

23...www.govexec.com   Big Data Challenge Debunking Myths

24...Military & Defense   Ryan Pickrell   27, Sept. 2019

25...USA Today Opinion Oct. 18, 2019 Opinion by Rita Nakashima & Ann Kansfield

26...www.vetdogs.org Smith Town, New York

27...Fox News Investigates   July 29, 2019

28...Guitar Heroes   NPR Weekend Addition Health Care   July 3, 2011

When our nation goes to war, everyone in uniform goes. Yes, the front-line soldier is at war, but so is everyone else in the military. Everything we do or fail to do can affect the life of a member of our team. It's horrible when a member of your team is killed, but it's also tough looking on a human being who is the enemy, shooting him and watching him die. War is full of stress.

We in uniform are comrades of all others in uniform—and we must stand with our brothers-and-sisters-in-arms. Some of us will suffer; some will not.

Prior to WWI war was not fought at night—as there were no portable lights good enough to fight by, so nights were for decompressing—and it worked. That's no longer true.

We must pay attention to our fellow warriors and help them identify any hidden wounds—and then stand with them as they heal.

– Denny Gillem

Jim Pidgeon was a US Navy Aviation Machinist 2nd Class from 1969 to 1973. He served as Flight Deck Trouble Shooter VAW-114, CVA-63 aboard the USS Kitty Hawk in the Tonkin Gulf Vietnam. He is a Life Member of AMVETS, DAV, VFW and AMERICAN LEGION. Jim is a Past AMVETS National Cmdr from 2015 to 2016. He is also the Co-founder of *22 Everyday Push Up Challenge.* He was formally recognized by President Trump in Louisville Kentucky on August 2019, for his dedication to raise awareness to eliminate veteran suicide.

Vietnam was unpopular, but American warriors don't choose the wars they fight in. They go where they are sent, trusting that the people they serve will value their sacrifice and their service.

"We know not of the future and cannot plan for it much. But we can hold our spirits and our bodies so pure and high, we may cherish such thoughts and such ideals, and dream such dreams of lofty purpose, that we can determine and know what manner of men [and women] we will be whenever and wherever the hour strikes that calls to noble action . . . NO MAN [OR WOMAN] BECOMES SUDDENLY DIFFERENT FROM HIS [OR HER] HABIT AND CHERISHED THOUGHT."

~ Joshua Chamberlain
Dedication of the 20th Maine
Monument, Gettysburg,
Pennsylvania   October 3, 1889

CHAPTER 12

THE "F" BOMB AND THE DEMISE OF CIVIL DISCOURSE

BY JACK GRUBBS

WENT TO A SMALL HIGH SCHOOL ON the outskirts of San Antonio, Texas. In those days, boys and girls got along well and respected each other to a high level. To the best of my recollection, neither gender swore in front of the other. Following basketball or football practice, some lightly salted language was passed around among the boys in the locker room – but never in front of a coach. I suspect the girls' use of foul language was much less than ours. I have always viewed that period of my life as "the halcyon days of youth." And, yes, we all had hormones. But we also had a culture of respecting the opposite sex and a modicum of discipline.

Frontlines of Freedom

I remember an incident in the spring of 1958 when I broke the code of conduct between male and female. During a lunch break a group of us, mostly boys, were in the parking lot shooting the bull. One of the few girls, Tina was her name, made a statement I considered somewhat obtuse. I rudely said to her, "Aw, knock it off Tina or I'll take you into the bushes." The word "f**k" was never uttered, but the implication was clear. That she was deeply embarrassed flew directly over my head.

The bell rang and we all made our way back into school. I was walking down the hall with two of my buddies when I felt a small tap on my shoulder. I turned around – "Wham!" she slapped me with every ounce of strength she could muster. As small as she was, she mustered a lot. I was stunned; I was embarrassed. My response was something to the effect, "Tina, you're right. I apologize." Tina, unlike too many people today, had a red line concerning civil behavior and discourse that she refused to allow others to cross. The blistering incident with Tina occurred over six decades ago; it seems as though it happened yesterday. Over the years her actions in the school hallway have affected my personal conduct with women in a profound manner.

Consider the following:

American Military Veterans

*"Congress shall make no law respecting
an establishment of religion, or
prohibiting the free exercise thereof;
or abridging the freedom of speech,
or of the press; or the right of the
people peaceably to assemble, and to
petition the Government for a redress of
grievances."*

The First Amendment to our Constitution is packed with principles written in hopes that the great experiment known as the United States would survive for centuries as a healthy institution of human freedom. To achieve "life, liberty, and the pursuit of happiness," the Founding Fathers added the words, "or abridging (deny; diminish; curtail; etc.) the freedom of speech." Underpinning the free speech portion of the First Amendment was the assumption that the electorate would be well informed and responsible. Many citizens of our country today are neither. The specific words above spell out the principle that, as a citizen of the United States, any American can speak his or her mind on any topic except shouting words such as "fire!" or exposing classified information.

My freedom of speech is the same as yours. If I say "Go F**k yourself" (as Vice President Cheney said, on the Senate floor, to Senator Patrick Leahy following a confrontation over the Halliburton

Oil and Energy Company,) I have every right to do so. So do you. Of course, there may be undesired consequences for making such statements. Vice President Joe Biden exclaimed to President Barack Obama, "This is a big f**king deal!" over an open microphone at the signing of President Obama's Affordable Care Act (Obamacare). Not to be outdone, President Donald Trump added a full portion of vulgarity upon entering the political arena.

In the cases just mentioned, neither Cheney nor Biden uttered their words with the intention of having those statements reach the ears of a national audience. During his campaign, President Donald Trump used four- and five-letter words at large rallies, providing viewers and readers language that was both astounding and troubling. Since his election, President Trump's vulgarity has ebbed significantly (although his less vulgar words are still inappropriate). Such is not the case for someone like Congresswoman Rashida Tlaib (D-MI). At her 2018 post-election victory party, she told a very enthusiastic throng of supporters,

> *"People love you and you win. And when your son looks at you and says, 'Momma, look, you won. Bullies don't win.' And I said, 'Baby, they don't. Because we're going to go in*

there and we're going to impeach the motherf**ker . . ."

The news media picked it up and spread it across the country. The statement in itself is offensive, inflammatory, crude, coarse, vile, disrespectful and on ad-infinitum. If spoken to a child (which she did) the words are also dangerous. What has she deposited into the mind of a young boy other than white-hot hate? The big difference between Congresswoman Tlaib and the words of Vice Presidents Biden and Cheney is that, from my foxhole, she did intend her words to be heard. Her words describe just how far our national discourse and culture have declined over the last sixty years.

I am not writing this chapter to wage war on Congresswoman Tlaib, but I will use her statement as the endpoint of a continuum beginning in the 1960's that has shown the not-so-slow decline of the civil discourse of our national culture. Just a notch above her were the words of former Congressman Beto O'Rourke. His spewing the F-bomb and his selling of t-shirts with "f**ked up" come across as a little boy having a meltdown. Worse than that, his producing t-shirts with "I f**ked up" written multiple times on the front will, at least in some circles, give the word an undeserved strength to drive American culture lower than ever before. I could list a string of names of politicians from both parties who seem to have no regard for civility in using the English language. But politicians aren't the only villains. Return with me to the 1960's.

Probably the most troubling event for Americans in 1960 was the simmering conflict in South Vietnam. The United States government feared the "domino" effect of countries falling to communism and supported the government of South Vietnam and its leader, Ngo Dinh Diem. At that point in our history, the use of "f**k" in a public space was basically zero. As the war grew in scope – and in casualties – the use of the word began to creep into the vocabulary of students pro-testing the war and the draft. In addition to "Hell no, I won't go" came signs of "Killing for Peace is like f**king for Virginity." The word's usage began to grow. I can't say to what degree or how causal the F-bomb was to our values, or our values to the F-bomb. It's similar to the question, "was it the chicken or the egg? One thing is certain: there is a linkage between societal decline and the increased frequency of the word "f**k" in public. Speaking of using the word in public, recently my wife and I sat down at a patio table at our favorite Mexican restaurant. To our left was a family with two small children, about seven and eight years old. To our right was a table with three college women. Their use of "F**k this" and "F**k that" seemed to flow like water from a hose. What a difference in language use since the good old days. Knowing the family was disturbed by the language. I did ask the young ladies to refrain from using the word. They were nice enough to refrain from the coarse language and left shortly thereafter. The really disappointing part of the incident was that the young women did not seem to even notice they were using foul language.

Returning to 1960, another phenomenon occurred: the introduction of "the pill." The ability to control a woman's reproductive cycle was the harbinger of many changes related to her lifestyle. The conception aspect of the pill certainly led to different social mores such as relationships with men, the family, pre-marital sex, the confrontation with religion, and the workplace (business, academia, science, politics). The newfound security of the pill to protect them from pregnancy gave women equality in the home. As women moved more into the workplace, conversations and interactions with men became rougher than prior to the pill. A major effect of the pill was the astounding change in lifestyle. Sexual freedom affected the family structure and family communications - today daycare centers are ubiquitous - delays in starting a family, moving in with one another rather than marrying. The level of discourse among and between men and women declined as well. Much like a parasite, the F-bomb attached itself to American culture.

By the end of the '60's the F-bomb had marched its way into the American mainstream. Panning the student sections for the 1969 football game between the University of Michigan Wolverines and the Ohio State University Buckeyes, the television crew made the mistake of doing so live. As the students were cheering at the camera, one student held up a sign reading, "F**k Michigan." From "Hell No, I won't go" to "F**k Michigan," the use of the F-bomb was here to stay. The big difference with today is that its public use in the '60's, '70's, and '80's was relegated to people with a small vocabulary or lack of self-esteem – many are now in leadership positions across the United States. Enter Hip-Hop and the film industry.

The next phenomenon is Hip-Hop and Rap. Most people would say Rap grew out of the Hip-Hop culture. As for Hip-Hop, a message is meant to be sent describing "life on the block." Lyrics of Hip-Hop are by far the most vulgar of all music genres. It is the most misogynistic music ever written. Hip-Hop represents a bifurcation point in which most other music, especially Country and Western, has maintained a relatively benign face. Hip-Hop, by comparison, is written to inflame and simultaneously tell a story of life in "the hood." The words "F**k, f**king," and "motherf**ker" are tossed around in an almost infinite manner.

The same is true for every other crude word one can spew. The problem of Hip-Hop - with its unending use of these words – is its opposition to having a healthy society where men and women of all races, ethnic backgrounds, geographic homesteads, and sexual orientation, can respect each other. It must include an elevation in the quality and meaning of the spoken word. While Hip-Hop is often filled with wonderful rhythm, its message wants to keep people, mostly women, in the bonds of despair.

The film industry can challenge Hip-Hop for the furthest fall in values. Clark Gable's famous words, "Frankly, my dear, I don't give a damn," in the 1939 classic, *Gone with the Wind*, pale in comparison to the 506 F-bombs uttered in the 2013 movie, *The Wolf of Wallstreet*. The often-changing rating guide uses the following:

G – All ages admitted.

PG - Parental Guidance Suggested.

PG-13 – Parents are urged to be cautious.

R – Restricted. Requires accompanying parent or adult guardian.

NC-17 Adults only. No one 17 and Under admitted.

The problem with the rating scheme shown above is that the separation lines between each category are often blurred. What one person judges as

"R" might be "PG-13" to another. The rule of the bottom line (e.g., profit) has led to (1) some people being very wealthy and (2) many patrons spending money on a prurient product.

We can bundle many things under the heading "technology." The laptop, personal computers, MacBook, Facebook, Instagram and other forms of technology advancement, add up to being a blessing and a curse. As a blessing, everything from infrastructure to aircraft design has been made easier and more efficient by the use of technology. Conversely, the word "f**k" makes it simple to view that which destroys family after family – pornography. On a hunch, I typed in "f**k" into the Google search engine. In half a second, 1,210,000,000 hits were listed. The average age of a child's first encounter with pornography is 11. What does such a statistic imply? There is a catastrophe on the horizon if pornography is not defeated. The case to be made is this: F-bombs will clutter the streets of towns, cities, and farms throughout the country until people realize just how far our society has declined while our use of the word has multiplied. Left, right, independent, it matters not what your political views are. What does matter is the future of American culture.

We are now in the first quarter of the 21st century. Today, civility in all areas of endeavor is conditional in its execution. If you agree with me,

American Military Veterans

I love you; if you disagree with me, you are the scum of the Earth and a "f**king idiot. The United States must clean up its act, specifically among its leaders. And how do we accomplish such a feat? Right now, I must agree with Professor Wilfred M. McClay, who, in his address of July 17, 2019 at the Allan P. Kirby Jr. Center for Constitutional Studies and Citizenship, stated:

> ". . . each of us is born into a world
> that we did not make, and it is only
> with the greatest effort, and often
> at very great cost, that we are ever
> able to change that world for the
> better."

Religious groups, parents, teachers, military and corporate leaders, and every other American must understand the price we all pay for our divided and non-civil society today, a battered but still beautiful institution. Today might just be a good time to reflect on what you have – and have not – done to bring our country back from a cultural abyss. You can build strategies for success and, starting with your ability to communicate with others in a civil manner, make our world a better place to live. Be the standard for civility. Be an American.

> *Ethics: "What you do for others who
> can do absolutely nothing for you".*

Quotes on Civility

"Be civil to all, sociable to many, familiar with few, friend to one, enemy to none."

– Benjamin Franklin

"Every action done in company ought to be with some sign of respect to those that are present."

– George Washington

"When once the forms of civility are violated, there remains little hope of return to kindness or decency."

– Samuel Johnson

"I know no religion that destroys courtesy, civility, and kindness."

– William Penn

"We hear a great deal about the rudeness of the rising generation. I am an oldster myself and might be expected to take the oldsters' side, but in fact I have been far more impressed by the bad manners of parents to children than by those of children to parents."

– C.S. Lewis

Jack Grubbs enlisted in the Army in 1959 and received a Bachelor of Science degree from the United States Military Academy, a Master of Science degree in Engineering from Princeton University, and a Ph.D. in Civil Engineering from Rensselaer Polytechnic Institute. His military career spanned four decades taking him to the United States, Vietnam, Korea, and Okinawa. Following the military he spent eight years on the faculty and administrative staff of Tulane University. In 2006, Jack became a principal owner of Simon-Meyer Charlotte, LLC, a construction-consulting firm. He has authored two leadership books, *Leadership: Taking the High Road*, and *The Legacy of Maggie Dixon*; a mystery trilogy occurring in Texas; and a 50-year history of a unique military organization, the Joint Communications Support Element (JSCE), *The Voice Heard Around the World*. His greatest accomplishment was convincing Judy Schultz of Bangor, Pennsylvania to join him on an incredible journey through life. They have three beautiful daughters, seven wonderful granddaughters, and an unstoppable grandson – appropriately named Jack.

The Grant Memorial is located at Union Square, which also is part of the Capitol Reflecting Pool. This picture shows part of the memorial, The Artillery Group, which shows a caisson carrying three artillerymen, pulled by three horses. Mounted on the left horse is the guidon (flag) carrier who is signaling a sharp right wheel.

"We hold these truths to be self-evident, that all men are created equal, that they are endowed by their Creator with certain unalienable Rights, that among these are Life, Liberty and the pursuit of Happiness. — That to secure these rights, Governments are instituted among Men, deriving their just powers from the consent of the governed,"

– 2nd paragraph of the Declaration of Independence

CHAPTER 13

FREEDOM WITHOUT GOD

BY CHRIS MORAN

RECLAIMING OUR NATION UNDER GOD

CAN WE TRULY HAVE FREEDOM without God? The founders of this exceptional country recognized God as the true source of freedom and the current secularist push to eradicate God from the culture completely debases America's founding that made this country great. This will result in a decline in the country's morals and standards where each person determines what is right for themselves. People will be elected who will slowly take more and more of our freedoms away as the government enlarges, and is increasingly relied upon as the answer for individual and social problems, making this country unrecognizable compared to what it once was.

It is not possible to have freedom without God and our founders knew that. That is why they created a unique limited government that only works when governing an internally restrained people that only Christianity can produce and American law reflects the bedrock of Judeo-Christian values this country was founded upon. If the founders viewed God as important in establishing a nation, then every American should view it the same and protect it, Christian or non-Christian.

In order to reverse this secularist trend to return to and protect our founding on God, Americans need to look back at the founders' view of God and His role in government and life, align their lives in accordance with God's teachings and defend the founders' intent in the culture wherever possible. America cannot exist as it does today without God as the cultural foundation. This chapter will look at two of America's founding documents, quotes from the founding fathers that give us insight as to the background and intent of what they wrote, the backwards use of the separation of church and state, and how to stem the progress of secularism and bring this country back to one nation truly under God.

AMERICA IS EXCEPTIONAL!

American Military Veterans

... BECAUSE OF GOD

America is the greatest country on the face of the earth! It is truly exceptional! The things this country has accomplished in the medical field, space, aviation, military and energy is incredible! We are the best in every area! American exceptionalism is something that should be taught in every school, kindergarten through college. But, why us? Why this country? What makes us different from all the other 195 countries? At an age of 233 years old, the U.S. constitution is the oldest surviving national constitutional document in the world.[1] Mila Versteeg, Professor of Law at University of Virginia, and Emily Zackin, Professor of Political Science at John Hopkins University, state in their article, *American Constitutional Exceptionalism Revisited*, there are distinct differences in our Constitutional text compared to other countries' governing documents, such as the document's conciseness and the glaring exclusion of specific socioeconomic rights.[2] Then they make an interesting statement. They say "these differences have led many to conclude that there is something

---

1-Versteeg, Mila, and Emily Zackin. 2014. "American Constitutional Exceptionalism Revisited." University of Chicago Law Review 81 (4): 1641–1707. http://search.ebscohost.com.aufric.idm.oclc.org/login. aspx?direct=true&db=aph&AN =100143453&site=ehost-live&scope=site
2-IBID

different about Americans and their vision of government that is reflected in their very different Constitution.[3] They don't say it, but what is different about Americans was this: the founders' view of God. This is the underpinning of American exceptionalism. If the founders didn't view God as the sole source of freedom and the sustainer of it, this country would look entirely different. Ravi Zacharias says there is no other religion or world view than the Judeo-Christian world view that would have resulted in a product of what we have in America today.[4] The statements and conversations of our founding fathers, the direct and indirect use of God in the text of the Declaration of Independence and our Constitution reveal why America is exceptional.

GOD IN OUR FOUNDING DOCUMENTS

A brief look at both the Declaration of Independence and the Constitution will show multiple direct and indirect references to God which gives us insight to what the founders thought about the role of God in life and our government. In the Declaration of Independence, it states:

> "...we hold these truths to be self-evident, that all men are created

3-IBID
4-Zacharias, Ravi. "Just Thinking Podcast." Just Thinking Podcast(blog). RZIM, May 11, 2019. https://www.rzim.org/listen/just-thinking/pursuit-of-truth-part-1.

equal, that they are endowed
by their Creator with certain
unalienable rights, that among
these are Life, Liberty and the
pursuit of Happiness.—That to
secure these rights, Governments
are instituted among Men, deriving
their just powers from the consent
of the governed."

Later, after the founders list their grievances against Great Britain, they write:

"...appealing to the Supreme Judge
of the world" and "with a firm
reliance on the protection of divine
Providence, we mutually pledge to
each other our Lives, our Fortune
and our sacred Honor." [5]

In the Constitution, there are three references to Christianity and God, two direct and one indirect. The first is a direct reference is the first amendment,

"Congress shall make no law
respecting an establishment of
religion, or prohibiting the free

5- "Declaration of Independence: A Transcription." National Archives and Records Administration. National Archives and Records Administration. Accessed November 3, 2019. https://www.archives.gov/founding-docs/declaration-transcript.

exercise thereof..."

Before the final wording of this amendment was decided upon, George Mason, also the "Father of the Bill of Rights," sent a Master Draft to General John Lamb with amendment 20 that proposed not to favor a certain Christian sect, not a certain religion. It stated:

> *"That Religion or the Duty which*
> *we owe to our Creator, and the*
> *manner of discharging it, can*
> *be directed only by Reason and*
> *Conviction, not by Force or*
> *violence, and therefore all men have*
> *an equal, natural and unalienable*
> *right to the free exercise of religion,*
> *according to the dictates of*
> *conscience; and that no particular*
> *sect or society of Christians ought*
> *to be favored or established by law*
> *in preference to others."*

This provides insight in the discussion surrounding this first amendment and that they weren't talking about religion in general. The founders were mainly thinking of the different denominations within the Christian religion, because, at that time, all 13 American colonies had some form of state-sponsored religion.[6] The second is an indi-

6-https://Undergod.procon.org/view.resource.
php?resourceID=000069

rect reference.

Article one section seven says

> "...If any Bill shall not be returned
> by the president within ten days
> (Sundays excepted)..."

Sundays were excepted because the government was off that day because of the traditional Christian observance of the sabbath being Sunday as it is today. Lastly, there is a direct reference in the format in which they wrote the date before the signatures.

It stated

> "the seventeenth Day of September
> in the Year of our Lord..."

These three examples fly in the face of those who say government and states should be godless, because the constitution is a godless document. They completely ignore all the surrounding context that point to the importance of God in the view of the founding fathers. There is no other world view that "hold these truths to be self-evident, that all men are created equal" not even secularism. Christianity and God permeated the culture and some of the lives of the signers of the constitution. Newt Gingrich, in his book *Trump's America*, said that of the 89 signers of the Declaration of Independence and the Constitution, almost a dozen were ordained ministers, studied theology, preachers, militia chaplains or officers of national Bible societies.[7] Many say that the majority of the others identified as Christian or were influenced by Christianity. Yet, religion and God in our culture has been under attack from the beginning, and it still is today.

SEPARATION OF CHURCH AND STATE TURNED ON ITS HEAD

There is a very concerted effort to attack America's Christian founding, and the majority of this attack stakes its validity on a statement made by Thomas Jefferson. Article one of the Bill of Rights which includes the establishment clause, says that "Congress shall make no law respecting an establishment of religion, or prohibiting the free exercise thereof…" Responding to a letter from the Danbury Baptist Association, Thomas Jefferson made the statement "…thus building a wall of separation between Church and State." This phrase has been taken out of context and is used largely to attempt to eliminate God completely, regardless of the verbiage of the first amendment and the intention of the founding fathers that wrote this. The is what activist judges and organizations, such as The Freedom From Religion Foundation (FFRF) nonprofit, use as they target individuals, businesses,

7-Gingrich, Newt. Trump's America. New York, NY: Hatchet Book Group, Inc., 2018.

schools, public grounds, courthouses, graduations, high school ballgames, etc., to eliminate anything they can that relates to God. As a matter of fact, the FFRF states that their purpose is to uphold the "separation of state and church and to educate the public on matters relating to non-theism."[8] That is not consistent with the founders' views. Nowhere does it say that a citizen should be restricted in certain instances. It was never designed to keep the influences of religion out of public life.

John Adams said "our Constitution was made only for a moral and religious people. It is wholly inadequate for the government of any other."[9] Yet these groups who stand for separation of church and state hijack Thomas Jefferson's statement for their own purposes. They are essentially forcing their non-religion on the rest of society, many of whom are religious. And there are judges who side with them and cite this phrase in their court decisions. What is ironic, and, separation of church and state supporters fail to mention, is that as governor of Virginia, Thomas Jefferson proposed bills that allowed him to appoint a day of fasting or thanks-

8-"What Is the Foundation's Purpose? - Freedom From Religion Foundation." What is the Foundation's purpose? - Freedom From Religion Foundation. Accessed November 3, 2019. https://ffrf.org/faq/item/14999-what-is-the-foundations-purpose.

9-From John Adams to Massachusetts Militia, 11 October 1798," Founders Online, National Archives, accessed September 29, 2019, https://founders.archives.gov/documents/Adams/99-02-02-3102.

giving.[10]   He even proposed the state seal depict Moses holding out his hands over the sea that overwhelmed Pharaoh, likening it to the American Revolution.[11]   At the end of his second inaugural address he encouraged Americans to seek "the favor of that Being in whose hands we are, who led our forefathers, as Israel of old…"[12]   Furthermore, two days after Thomas Jefferson made this statement, he attended a church service conducted in the House of Representatives! Would that go untested today? It's clear Thomas Jefferson did not mean for religion to be completely eradicated from government and public life. If it was okay then, why can't our courthouses or public places have the Ten Commandments, a nativity, or a cross? We have to return to the original founders' intent as close as possible and protect it if we want to be a great nation under God.

WE HAVE TO HAVE GOD
THE DEFINER OF TRUTH

After briefly looking at a few of our founding documents, the founders' conversations surrounding article one, and their statements on religion, it is clear that God and religion need to remain in the

10-Hall, Mark David. "Did America Have a Christian Founding?" The Heritage Foundation, June 7, 2011. https://www.heritage.org/political-process/report/did-america-have-christian-founding.
11-IBID
12-IBID

fabric of our culture. Then why do the secularists want to eliminate Judeo-Christian standards that clearly benefit society and have made this country great and distinguishable from any other? It's safe to say that everyone would want a society where all people are seen as equal, that treats others how they want to be treated, or and when people act with selflessness and humility. How about no killing, no stealing, no adultery, no lying about your neighbor, no coveting? That's good for society, right? They want the benefits of a Christian culture, but without God.

The FFRF website claims they were the "first ones to speak out for humane treatment of the mentally ill, for abolition of capital punishment, women's right to vote, death with dignity for the terminally ill, the right to choose contraception, sterilization and abortion and to end slavery."[13] By what truth can they make this support for these absolute standards they claim they are for? If there is no God, who makes the standards for right and wrong? Why is it a woman's right to vote? Why should there be dignity in death? Why is slavery wrong? If there is no God, there is no moral law. Morality is then defined by each person. Frederick Nietzche, a German atheist philosopher said "words, like a hall of mirrors, reflect only each other and in the end,

---

13-"About FFRF - Freedom From Religion Foundation." About FFRF - Freedom From Religion Foundation. Accessed November 3, 2019. https://ffrf.org/about.

point to the condition of their users, without having established anything about the way things really are."[14] The problem of there being no God is that you end up with 7.6 billion relative truths that end up pointing back to the one attempting to define truth and not even getting close to describing the way things really are. Truth is reality the way God sees it, and that cannot be determined by any one of us. Truth has to come from something higher than ourselves. In his speech at Notre Dame on October 14, 2019, Attorney General (AG) Barr was talking about moral values and that James Madison's statement of self-government really meant "the capacity of each individual to restrain and govern themselves … by freely obeying the dictates of inwardly-possessed and commonly-shared moral values … that must rest on authority independent of men's will—they must flow from a transcendent Supreme Being."[15] This internal restraint is what allows this limited government to work. To have that restraint, we have to have God in our culture and allow the instructions of our Creator to permeate our lives and live according to godly values, because our founders acknowledged Him as our Creator and the Creator sets the rules, and defines

14-Philip Novak, The Vision of Nietzsche (Vega, 2003), 8-11
15-Barr, William P. Accessed October 14, 2019. https://www.justice.gov/opa/speech/attorney-general-william-p-barr-delivers-remarks-law-school-and-de-nicola-center-ethics.

morality. Ravi Zacharias says that we are naïve to think that we can exist in the state that we are in or improve our society without God. "Nature abhors a vacuum. There are other worldviews that will see this vacuum and storm in… and as a secularist society, we will never have the moral power to withstand that movement and our nation will crumble."[16] Ronald Reagan said, "If we ever forget that we are one nation under God, then we will be a nation gone under."

THE CRACKS OF A GODLESS CULTURE

As a result of this concerted effort we have begun to see the ramifications of a godless culture. Since Roe v. Wade, the acceptance of abortions and late-term abortions seem to be more common, even state leaders being ok with terminating a baby after he or she is born! There is an increase of government dependency and a lack of self-responsibility which is a ration of slavery and an element of socialism seeping in.[17] This slow creep towards socialism is revealed in areas where we look to government to be the answer. Instead of dealing with the underlying causes ourselves, we look to the State to be the alleviator of bad consequences.

16-Zacharias, Ravi. "Just Thinking Podcast." Just Thinking Podcast(blog). RZIM, May 11, 2019. https://www.rzim.org/listen/just-thinking/pursuit-of-truth-part-1.
17-Holmes, Phillip. "The Heart of Socialism." Desiring God, March 17, 2016. https://www.desiringgod.org /articles/the-heart-of-socialism.

We call on the State to mitigate the social costs of personal misconduct and irresponsibility.[18] For example, "the reaction to growing illegitimacy or unwanted pregnancy is not sexual responsibility, but abortion. The reaction to drug addiction is safe injection sites."[19] In his speech, AG Barr also mentions the breakdown of the family as a result of beginning to eliminate God from our culture. This is probably the most detrimental consequence to society. The statistics are heartbreakingly staggering!

Fatherless children account for 63% of youth suicides.

- 90% of homeless/runaway children.

- 80% of rapists with anger problems.

- 71% of high school dropouts.

- More likely to do drugs, commit crime and be sexually active outside of marriage therefore repeating the cycle.

- There are 64.3 million fathers nationwide and only 26.5 million are married and raising their own children.

- There are 2.5 million single fathers, 42% are divorced.

18-Barr, William P. Accessed October 14, 2019. https://www.justice.gov/opa/speech/attorney-general-william-p-barr-delivers-remarks-law-school-and-de-nicola-center-ethics.
19-IBID

- Of all single parents living with their children, 18% of them are men.[20]

This is where the battle for America rages, and it starts with individuals and families to fight it. There is a reason God has set standards for relationships prior to and after marriage and guidelines for how the family is supposed to function. Attorney General Barr says, "violations of these moral laws have bad, real-world consequences for man and society."[21] Rules and guidance from God are not arbitrary, there are real natural blessings and consequences for following God's standard of living, and it benefits society as a whole when they're followed. If not followed, we may not pay the price immediately, but over time the harm is real. Religion helps promote moral discipline within society because man is fallen. The fact is that no secular creed has emerged capable of performing the role of religion,[22] and no amount of laws can have the same effect on a person that religion does. That is why it is important to elect the type of leaders who recognize the critical importance of, and to keep God in our culture.

20-"Statistics." The Fatherless Generation, April 28, 2010. https://thefatherlessgeneration.wordpress.com/statistics/.
21-Barr, William P. Accessed October 14, 2019. https://www.justice.gov/opa/speech/attorney-general-william-p-barr-delivers-remarks-law-school-and-de-nicola-center-ethics.
22-IBID

THE IMPORTANCE OF OUR LEADER'S
RECOGNITION OF GOD

This next election in 2020 is the most important election of our lifetime. The difference between President Trump and the Democrat candidates at this time could not be wider. It is extremely important to elect a president that will protect religious liberty. Regardless of what kind of person you think he is or if you don't like what he tweets, President Trump has repeatedly said and emphasized the importance of being a nation under God, and his words, policies and the people he appoints backs that up. For example, in his speech on the National Day of Prayer in 2018, President Trump said "...we join together to offer gratitude for our many blessings and to acknowledge our need for divine wisdom, guidance and protection. Prayer, by which we affirm our dependence on God, has long been fundamental to our pursuit of freedom...
"[23]   On the National Day of Prayer in 2019, he said "...we proudly come together as one nation under God" and mentions the importance of saying Christmas instead of Happy Holidays. He also said "we are building a culture that cherishes the dignity and worth of human life. Every child, born and

23-Trump, Donald. "National Day of Prayer 2018." National Day of Prayer 2018. Accessed November 3, 2019. https://www.whitehouse.gov/briefings-statements/remarks-president-trump-national-day-prayer/.

unborn, is a sacred gift from God."[24] Additionally, he is the only U.S. president in history and the first leader at the U.N. to speak on religious liberty in the world, because he, like the founders, understands that our freedom originates from God, not the government. He has also appointed many originalist judges on the Supreme Court and courts throughout the country. Aside from judges, President Trump has also made excellent appointments in Mike Pompeo as the Secretary of State, a born-again Christian and AG Bill Barr, a staunch advocate for religious liberty, vowing to protect religious liberty throughout the country.

IT STARTS WITH YOU AND ME

Americans need to elect local, state, and federal leaders who understand our founders' dependence on God for our freedom for our country's future and the importance of religious liberty in order to stave off the decline. But that alone will not bring America back to God. It starts with each individual person first, conducting their lives in accordance to our Maker's standards, and influencing the circles they live in and then stand up, support, and vote for those who protect God in our culture. May God have mercy on us and give courage to those leaders who defend God in our culture and the freedom of religion in every corner of our nation. May God bless America now and for the generations to come.

24-IBID

About the Founders

Our founders were mostly Christian, but some were not. However, when beginning a new group or nation it is necessary to establish a value set or culture for those people. Our founders wisely selected Judeo-Christian values for our nation.

When our nation divided during the Civil War the Rebels fighting song was *Dixie*. What was the Union's equivalent? *The Battle Hymn of the Republic*. It begins, "My eyes have seen the glory of the coming of the Lord…" It is blatantly Christian in every verse. Ours was and was intended to be a Christian nation.

The Judeo-Christian culture and ethics helped us become the most wealthy and powerful nation in the world, and in that role we have helped people in a great many nations around the world. And a result of our helping others was not the growth of our nation through colonialism.

Today, the only acceptable value is to have no values. To stand up for any standard is to invite name calling, ie., bigot or some kind of -phobe. This is not to say that we require anyone to belong to any particular religion; it is to say that we require everyone to act decently. We Americans need to take back our nation's culture by returning to our Judeo-Christian values.

Chris is 35 years of age and happily married with 4 kids. He has served in the U.S. Air Force for 9 years on Active Duty and is currently a pilot in the Air Force Reserves and at a civilian airline. He has a strong Judeo-Christian background and has been active at a local church his entire life. He believes that a strong family is the bedrock and strength of our country and the breakdown of the family is the source of the current decline in American culture. Therefore, he has dedicated himself the past seven years to participating in and leading small groups for young married couples that focus on strengthening marriages and families.

"*Four score and seven years ago our fathers brought forth on this continent, a new nation, conceived in Liberty, and dedicated to the proposition that all men are created equal.*

Now we are engaged in a great civil war, testing whether that nation, or any nation so conceived and so dedicated, can long endure. We are met on a great battle-field of that war. We have come to dedicate a portion of that field, as a final resting place for those who here gave their lives that that nation might live. It is altogether fitting and proper that we should do this."

— Abraham Lincoln
Opening to the Gettysburg Address

In this temple
as in the hearts of the people
for whom he saved the union
The memory of Abraham Lincoln
is enshrined forever

democracy[dih-mok-ruh-see]
1a: government by the people
especially: rule of the majority b: a
government in which the supreme
power is vested in the people
and exercised by them directly
or indirectly through a system of
representation usually involving
periodically held free elections
— *Merriam-Webster*
Dictionary

CHAPTER 14

NOT A DEMOCRACY

BY DENNY GILLEM

THREE HUNDRED YEARS ago most of our East Coast was composed of British Colonies. When the citizens of the colonies became tired of being exploited by the Mother Country they revolted—that's the American Revolution. The Continental Congress passed the Declaration of Independence on July 4, 1776. The colonies weren't even a country then and had no army, yet they declared war on the most powerful nation on earth, Great Britain—a nation that had an army here and a fleet off-shore. And we won our independence.

Frontlines of Freedom

The thirteen former colonies all wanted to become independent nations, but they realized that together they could better defend themselves against European powers. The states knew they could take care of themselves and their people; they created a national government to do for them things that could better be done at the national level—like raise an army, issue currency, and conduct foreign relations. They never, ever intended for the national government to be very powerful, and never wanted it to meddle in State business. This is written into the Constitution. Article 1, Section 8 of the Constitution gives Congress the authority to do certain things; Article 1, Section 10 lists the things the States may not do. And the Tenth Amendment states that all power not given to the Congress nor prohibited to the States shall remain with the States and the people.

While, logically, the Constitution was written as a legal document to create our nation, a legal document says what it says and doesn't say what it doesn't say. However, there are those who believe that the Constitution is a "living document." It's meaning changes with time—and the Supreme Court (and other courts) decide what it means now. The Living Document perspective is what is being and has been used by our government for generations. This means that none of our rights is dependable. If the Court says that 'freedom of speech" really means that we are free to say what the government wants us to say—then that's what it means. Regardless of where you stand in the Pro-Life/Pro-Choice issue, there is not a word or a hint of sex or reproduction in our Constitution—yet abortion was declared to be a constitutionally protected right.

The States wanted to be sure that each state would always have a say in how the national government functioned. They did not want the large-population states to dominate the other states. Thus, they created the Electoral College; this ensures that the smaller states will not be ignored during elections. Remember that the States created the Federal Government—and they wanted the Federal Government to serve them—not vice-versa.

And the Constitution makes us a Republic—specifically not a democracy. We are, specifically, a Constitutional Republic. We are a nation ruled by law—not by the whims of men. The Constitution protects our rights. Very specifically, the Constitution protects the minorities from being oppressed by the majority. In a democracy the majority can vote to make you a slave or take your family or property from you—not so in our republic.

And our Republic won't work if we-the-people don't pay close attention to the people we elect.

Frontlines of Freedom

Most Americans can't even name five elected officials (of the several dozen) that they voted for. We need to know who the candidates are and support the ones who share our values; then we must hold them accountable—by following their activities and periodically contacting them. Yes, this is work, but it's our nation, and we're responsible for keeping it well run.

Please, read our founding documents—the Declaration of Independence and the Constitution—neither is very long. Ensure every member of your family has knowledge of what these documents say. Ask candidates for office about their knowledge of them and willingness to stand up for them. The Republic can only last if all citizens actually care about our national government and hold the elected officials there accountable.

Lieutenant Colonel Dennis J. Gillem is a 1964 graduate of the United States Military Academy at West Point, and a Vietnam combat veteran. He served two tours in Vietnam as a company grade officer where he received seven US awards for valor. After a distinguished military career he retired and now lives in Michigan with his wife and is an Adjunct Professor of Political Science.

LTC Gillem hosts the nationally syndicated military talk radio show, *Frontlines of Freedom*, which is heard every weekend nation-wide. Go to www.frontlinesoffreedom.com for local station listings and for podcasts.

Frontlines of Freedom

A Gift from the Founders

In a democracy the majority rules. The majority can take your property or family away from you or make you a slave. There are no restrictions on what the majority may do.

This is NOT the CASE in a CONSTITUTIONAL REPUBLIC.

In this case the citizens have the rule of law, not of men. The Constitution protects the minority from oppression by the majority.

The terms Muslim or Islamic world refer to all those (Muslim majority) nations who adhere to the religion of Islam, or to societies where Islam is practiced. All Muslims look for guidance to the Quran and believe in the prophetic mission of Muhammad, but disagreements on other matters have led to appearance of different religious schools and branches within Islam. The nation states that emerged in the post-colonial era have adopted a variety of political and economic models, and they have been affected by secular and as well as religious trends.

CHAPTER 15

THE ENEMY WITHIN

BY DAVE AGEMA

I WOULD LIKE TO START BY SAY-ing "that the Arab Muslim world, because of its religion (actually only 14% - 16% religion) and culture, is a natural threat to civilized people of the world, particularly Western Culture. The basic commandment of Islam is intolerance to anything non-Muslim. Islamic teaching is filled with hate against Jews, christians and infidels. The Koran is at odds with the Bible, our constitution and every other religion.

*"While Christians and Jews learn to
repair the world, love their enemy,
forgive those that trespass against them,
and turn the other cheek, Muslims are
taught to fight the infidels, to consider
them enemies of Allah."*
                    — Bridgette Gabriel

Most Christians, politicians and Americans
have no idea what the Koran or Sunna says; they
have become useful idiots, furthering the cause
of civilization jihad demanded by the Koran and
Sunna. (The Sunna is Mohammad's sayings and
biography, although he was illiterate. Others wrote
what he said and did.) The media is manipulating
a positive light for a dangerous enemy ... Islam.

*"Arabs are brainwashed by Arab media
who have stated the Jews make bread
with the blood of Muslims."*
                    — Bridgette Gabriel

Honesty and objectivity in their media could
get reporters legs broken, arms broken or get them
killed.

Islam teaches hate from birth. It's been said "
they are fed hatred by their mothers milk." Add to
this that there is NO free press in the Arab world,
and you have a recipe for indoctrination from birth

to death. Fear rules their media. Reporters must watch what they say about islam or pay the price. Even I have been put on a quasi hit list by CAIR for exposing the false teachings of Mohammad, the Koran and Sunna.

Our government leaders have been ignorant, and happy to be so. It took 911 for a wake up, but they went back to sleep. To put it another way, "when you put your head in the sand, all you do is make a big fat target out of your behind." The Muslim Brotherhood (MBH) has spent millions in 2017, 2018 and 2019 to persuade you they are peaceful, and they will continue to spend; its the Trojan horse in the US. Even worse, they now serve as congressman and congresswomen, swearing in on the very document, the Koran, that demands our destruction.

Let me give you a little US history concerning Islam and the MBH.

The 1991 MBH strategic plan called "the explanatory memorandum of the strategic goal of the north american' was discovered and it's goal was: to destroy western civilization from within via civilization jihad by the muslim brotherhood.

It was discovered in 2004 by the FBI, in a raid on Ismail Elbarassse's house in Virginia in a sub basement where 80 boxes of the archives of the MBH were found, detailing their goals for North America and particularly the United States.

Elbarasse was dressed as a female muslim with a burka taking pictures of the chesapeake bridge- highly suspicious and most likely for its destruction.

In these boxes were listed 29 MBH fronts: such as CAIR, ISNA, MSA, MMA and a host of others still operating in the USA.

GOALS

- Change Demographics (More Muslims In America (reproduce, impregnate, immigrate: legally and illegally.
- Change the legal system (sharia law).
- Change government and establishment of a caliphate (think one world government).
- Do not assimilate or cooperate to local culture.
- Ensuring we do not study their doctrine of sharia.
- Co-opting key leadership positions in politics (Michigan had a Muslim running for governor, and now the Muslim Tlaib is a congresswoman.) We have over 95 Muslims in office from congress to local government.)
- Gradually take over the religious and political systems, gradually at first, becoming more and more aggressive as numbers increase.

- Forcing sharia compliance at local levels.
- Subverting religious organizations. Think Christian.
- Claiming victimization; (they killed 300-500 million people.)
- Subverting the US education system via middle eastern studies programs and rewriting text books, teaching the 5 pillars of Islam to your kids.
- Condemning slander against islam.
- Confronting and denouncing western society, its laws and traditions.
- Demanding the right to practice sharia in segregated muslim enclaves.
- Demanding that sharia replace western law.

In short, it focuses on the settlement of North America by Islam, overtaking our culture and laws via islamic centers where radicalism is fostered with the goal of world domination so the "umma" is established. That is, we become a muslim nation under sharia law.

Refugee resettlement (called hijrah; it's what Muhammad did when he left Mecca for Medina-demanded by the trilogy which is the quran and Sunna which is the Sira (biography) and Hadith (Mohammad's sayings). ISIS stated they would use the refugee system to immigrate, which is mandated by the Koran called Hijrah.

Let's discuss this a bit. Mohammed tried to be a prophet to the Jews and Christians in Mecca, but they rejected him. He claimed Gabriel spoke to him and that he was the only prophet of allah. He had but a few converts over many years, so he fled to Medina. There he became a warlord and politician, killing and taking from any and all that would not convert or accept him. He eradicated the Jews who welcomed him as an immigrant in a few short years. He married 6-year-old Aisha, consummated the marriage at 9, stated that a new revelation had been given and that all the past writings that others wrote for him (because he was illiterate and couldn't read or write) were abrogated i.e., didn't count anymore. In short, join my group and kill and take from the infidel what you will.

He was involved with raids and killings nearly every 6 weeks of his later life and was poisoned by a woman. After his death, leaders of his own faith tried to kill all his progeny and make themselves the new ruler.

So, the goal of world domination is by jihad, the only true way to heaven continues ... to kill! We have been at war with Islam since 1776.

When america became a nation, the muslims in Tripoli declared war on America. They captured our ships, sailors and people and demanded payment for their return, which was about 20% of America's GDP. Jefferson and Adams met with the Imam in London, at which time the Imam said he could take what he wished from the infidels and would continue to do so. Jefferson printed 200 Korans so congress and Americans could see what a barbaric religion and way of life it was, and, as a result, the first Marine Corps and Navy was formed. It took several years, but we defeated the Muslims; however, they have been at war with America ever since in some form or another. The Marine Corps anthem still has in it "to the shores of Tripoli". We don't teach this in school. We should!

LETS TALK ABOUT THE REFUGEE ISSUE.

Before I start, please realize that each refugee will cost you $19,884 in cash assistance, welfare, food stamps, housing and medical aid, and, once naturalized, they petition to take in sons, daughters, brothers, sisters, etc. DNA testing has shown that as much as 90% of some family connections are a fraud. According to Brietbart, each Syrian refugee costs the American taxpayer $64,370 over the first 5 years. That's 12 times what it costs for them to stay in a neighboring Middle Eastern country. We're being had folks!

The refugee act of 1980 has created a very lucrative industry. Trump is trying to fix this, and it is long over due and this doesn't include the illegals crossing our borders.

The UN identifies the refugees, the U.S. State Department accepts them and places them directly into cities and towns with little notification, if any.

There are nine federal contractors and 350 subcontractors. Weekly meetings between the nine federal contractors and the state department determine which states get them. They are changing demographics folks and are not assimilating.

The contractors are paid per refugee. The US conference of catholic bishops received $2 billion over an 8-year-period, which is nearly 98% of their budget. The lutheran immigration and refugee service has received $295 million which is about 97% of their budget. So you can see, it's become a profitable business. Always follow the money in politics and government. They can get $2,200 per refugee, spend $200 of it on the refugee, give away $800 of goods or services that "others" donate and make $2,000 per refugee; this is big business, and lots of profit at our long-term expense. Shortly thereafter these agencies have no idea where they are or what they are doing. They are also not allowed to proselytize. This is a huge security risk.

HUMAN TRAFFICKING

Sharia law is involved in human trafficking

because of their low esteem for women.

A woman's testimony is half that of a mans.

If raped, a woman must produce four witnesses who viewed it to be exonerated. If not, the woman is stoned.

A man can have four wives (although Mohammad had between 7 and 11 at one time).

Mohammed said most people in hell will be women.

THEY PRACTICE FEMALE GENITAL MUTILATION.

Men can marry young girls (Mohammed married a 6-year-old and consummated it at age 9.)

BEATING OF WOMEN IS AUTHORIZED.

One million English girls have been raped by muslims, and sharia-compliant muslims are 170 times more likely to be involved in trafficking and grooming young girls for prostitution.

Sharia courts/councils are numbered between 30-80 in britain where sex crimes are condoned.

In the UK, 900 Syrians have been arrested for sex crimes and child abuse.

Syria and other sharia-compliant countries are some of the worst offenders of human trafficking.

Muslims are reproducing at 7 to 8.1 kids per family (a form of civilization jihad).

MICHIGAN REFUGEES

99% of the syrian refugees placed in Michigan in 2016 were muslim. Most are sunnis and they are mostly sharia compliant, and about 50% want to live under sharia. (Trojan horse within our country for civilization jihad.)

Michigan refugee numbers: In 2016 we got 3,548. 2016 was a 1,115 increase (43% increase) from 2015. (It's estimated that 1 in 5 are radicalized.)

Michigan was receiving 12% of the total number of Syrian refugees in the nation. It is foolish for our governor and legislature to accept this knowing ISIS has promised to use this for jihad.

The US is 4% of the world's population, but we take 20% of the refugees while Saudi Arabia takes none.

The refugee industry wanted to double these numbers in 2017 to get more money.

Hillary Clinton wanted to increase the numbers by 500% if she had won the election.

Saudi Arabia and other middle eastern countries have the money and space to accept thousands, but they accept none. Why? They are funding hijrah, a form of civilization jihad and want them in America. They have paid for over 2000 mosques to be built in America instead, to facilitate civilization jihad and flood america with muslims.

CIS (center for immigration studies) predicts a clinton presidency would have brought in one million more shariah-compliant muslims.

In the past, of all Syrian refugees taken, 99% were Sunni Muslims, and only eight were Christians. The UN High Commissioner for refugees picks the refugees, and he is pushing more to the US. They say they screen them, but our FBI director says this is a joke. Its really the UN and radical islamists that are choosing our refugee neighbors.

FOUR TACTICS OF ISLAM

- Multiplication of muslims via birthrates; they birth 7 to 8.1 Kids per family.
- Multiplication of muslims by immigration and illegal immigration. (80% we catch crossing the border that are not Hispanic are from Muslim countries. (According to Lt. General Jerry Boykin)
- Multiplication of muslim influence via political systems. Michigan had its first Muslim candidate for governor. Congresswoman and some towns are dominated by Muslims, like Hamtramck and Dearborn.

Another tactic is expulsion of non- muslims by force, rape, death, fear, slavery. Islam still practices slavery, especially in Africa.

The Hadith demands the following tactics: (what Muhammed said and did).

- To assemble
- To listen (don't question the faith)
- To immigrate
- To wage jihad
- To obey (religion of compulsion, but primarily a way of life and political system. Islam is only about 14-16% religion).

WHAT CAN YOU DO?

- First, get informed concerning islam. Study the Quran, Sira and the Hadith. It will open your eyes.

- State government must pass bills like ALAC (American Laws for American Courts), anti-sanctuary-city bills and resist sharia law in any way possible, and expose CAIR, ISNA, MSA, etc.

- State governments must stop illegal immigration and the refugee resettlements (Chamber of Commerce and the Farm Bureau push against stopping any form of cheap labor (follow the money). My e-verify bill was not passed out of committee, which would have prevented illegals from getting jobs.

- Before resettlement, cities and municipalities must be consulted and honor their requests to reject them.

- The refugee resettlement industry must be exposed for what they are doing to our safety, security and fiscal/physical health. (Many communicable diseases are re-entering our country.)

- Stop your city or town from being one of the "welcoming Michigan' partners which is a propaganda arm for the refugees.

- Corporations or businesses that promote mass immigration should be avoided. (Example: partnership for a new american economy- (an arm of soros).

- Write your legislators and especially governors who have openly asked for refugees, spoken well of CAIR and ISNA - both terror-funding organizations according to the holy land foundation trials of 2008.

The tears of jihad: deaths due to jihad over the last 1400 years. (These numbers are considerably larger now.)

Christians: 60 million
Hindus: 80 million
Buddhists: 10 million
African slave jihad: 120 million

Total= 270 million, Islam is a killing machine like no other. Some estimates are well over 500 million.

America is in crises and our congressman are either ignorant of the threat (which they should not be) or they are on the take to not be transparent with the populace. Too many can be swayed. Vote wisely!

Because I have spoken out concerning radical islam and have been misquoted by democrats and republicans, I and about 60 others have been placed on a quazi hit list for lone wolves by CAIR. This is unacceptable. It would be like me making a list of muslims I want taken out.

Its time we stop illegal immigration, the syrian refugee influx and learn that we are at war with a sly and dangerous enemy whose goal is destruction of America, Israel and desires world domination by force.

Folks, our political masters are destroying this country from within. It's time to elect new people who have integrity that can't be bought. Vote wisely! The enemy is within.

WHAT'S AN INFIDEL?

The author, Rick Mathes, who is a well-known leader in prison ministry wrote the following: "The man who walks with God always gets to his destination." If you have a pulse you have a purpose is his saying. Here is one of his speeches and experiences with a Muslim.

The Muslim religion is the fastest growing religion per capita in the US, especially in the minority races. Not the Catholics, not the Mormons. Last month I attended my annual training session that's required for maintaining my state prison security clearance. During the training session there was a presentation by three speakers representing the Roman Catholic, Protestant and Muslim faiths, who each explained their beliefs.

I was particularly interested in what the Islamic Imam had to say. The Muslim gave a great presentation of the basics of Islam, complete with a video. After the presentations, time was provided for questions and answers. When it was my turn, I directed my question to the Muslim and asked:

'Please, correct me if I'm wrong, but I understand that most Imams and clerics of Islam have declared a holy jihad [Holy war] against the infidels of the world and, that by killing an infidel, (which is a command to all Muslims) they are assured of a place in heaven. If that's the case, can you give me the definition of an infidel?'

There was no disagreement with my statements and without hesitation, he replied, "Nonbelievers."

I responded, 'So, let me make sure I have this

straight. All followers of Allah have been commanded to kill everyone who is not of your faith so they can have a place in heaven. Is that correct? The expression on his face changed from one of authority and command to that of a little boy who had just been caught with his hand in the cookie jar.'

He sheepishly answered ...."Yes" I then stated, 'Well, sir, I have a real problem trying to imagine the pope commanding all Catholics to kill those of your faith or Dr. Stanley ordering all Protestants to do the same in order to guarantee them a place in heaven!'

The Muslim was speechless.

I continued, 'I also have a problem with being your friend when you and your brother clerics are telling your followers to kill me! Let me ask you another question:

Would you rather have your Allah, who tells you to kill me in order for you to go to heaven, or my Jesus who tells me to love you because I am going to heaven and He wants you to be there with me?'

You could have heard a pin drop. Needless to say, the organizers and promoters of the 'Diversification' training seminar were not happy with my way of dealing with the Islamic Imam and exposing the truth about the Muslims' beliefs.

In 20 years there will be enough Muslim voters in the U.S. to elect the President !

I think everyone in the U.S. should be required to read this, but with the ACLU, there is no way this will be widely publicized, unless each of us sends it on!

This is your chance to make a difference.

FOR GOD'S SAKE...SEND THIS ON."

Author's Note:

Statistics cited in this chapter were taken from several sources and personal briefings by men like Lieutenant General Jerry Boykin and former PLO terrorist, Kamal Saleem.

The following books were also a wealth of knowledge:

Mohammad to ISIS by Robert Spenser

The Quran

The Sunna

The Holy Land Foundation Trial transcripts

The Blood of Lambs by Kamal Saleem

Never Surrender by Lt. General Jerry Boykin

About Islam

Most Muslims are of one of two denominations: Sunni (75–90%) and Shia. About 13% of Muslims live in Indonesia, the largest Muslim-majority country; 31% of Muslims live in South Asia; 20% in the Middle East–North Africa, where it is the dominant religion; and 15% in Sub-Saharan Africa and West Africa. Muslims are the overwhelming majority in Central Asia, the majority in the Caucasus and widespread in Southeast Asia. India is the country with the largest Muslim population outside Muslim-majority countries, having about 200 million Muslims. Sizeable Muslim communities are also found in the Americas, China, Europe, and Russia. Islam is the fastest-growing major religion in the world.

Retired Lt. Col David Agema (former fighter pilot). Former State Representative and RNC Committeeman for Michigan.

The federal government moved to Washington DC in the autumn of 1800. At that time the Capitol building was used for Sunday church services as well as for government functions. The initial religious services took place in the "hall" of the House in the north wing of the building.

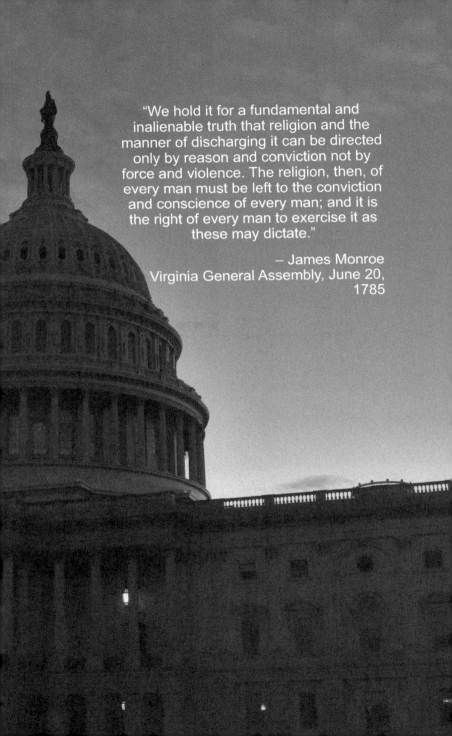

"We hold it for a fundamental and inalienable truth that religion and the manner of discharging it can be directed only by reason and conviction not by force and violence. The religion, then, of every man must be left to the conviction and conscience of every man; and it is the right of every man to exercise it as these may dictate."

– James Monroe
Virginia General Assembly, June 20, 1785

> *If Americans don't share common values, how can we be a unified nation?*
>
> *— Denny Gillem*

CHAPTER 16

THE DECAY OF THE WEST: DESTRUCTION BY MODERNITY AND MOHAMMEDANISM

BY BO BOLGIANO

WHILE NOT IMMEDIATELY apparent, this chapter is a military story because it is fundamentally a national security story. The United States of America is in a near-term existential fight for its survival as a free Constitutional Republic. The two threats are Modernity (also known as Progressivism, Leftism, Globalism, Socialism or Communism) and Mohammedans (also known as Radical Islamists.) We can lose our rights and maybe our lives much faster than the time it has taken to grow and nurture our Great Republic.

Any casual student of history can see the abysmal failures wrought by the governmental overreach of socialism: Soviet Russia, Chinese Communists, Cambodia, and Venezuela. Mohammedanism has brought us female genital mutilation, ongoing ethnic and religious cleansing, and destruction of all that is sacred to Christendom and the West. Those that deny this are either woefully ignorant or willfully blind or deceptive.

In the beautifully written book *The Great Heresies,* Hilaire Belloc identifies five major moral threats to Christendom: Arianism, Mohammedanism, Albigensianism, Protestantism and what Belloc labeled the "Modern Attack." Arianism and Albigensianism were disputes of the early Church concerning, respectively, the full divinity of Christ and the duality of good and evil in the Universe. These disputes were mostly resolved in the first millennium A.D. The violent upheavals between Catholics and Protestants were a problem primarily confined to Europe, and most of the bloody disputes between them were resolved after the Peace of Westphalia that capped the Thirty Years War.

The intellectual and spiritual rift between Roman Catholicism and Protestantism is still ongoing, yet it is a dispute that often fills pages with beautiful prose like that of John Henry Cardinal Newman. As a Roman Catholic, I pray for this split to be mended, with all Christian Churches coming together again under the guidance of Peter's successor. Whether that happens in my lifetime is not an existential threat to the West. Nor are the existence of practicing Jews, Hindus and Buddhists. That leaves Mohammedanism and Modernity as the unresolved and ever festering dangers to the good (Godly) order and moral freedoms of the West's Judeo-Christian heritage so beautifully exemplified in the Declaration of Independence and our Republic's other founding documents.

With its Judeo-Christian roots, a truly free and classically liberal[1] society – one that respects private property rights and allows men to freely follow God's Grace that is deep in every person's heart – is the least imperfect of man-made societies. It is the society envisioned by our Founding Fathers as so clearly set forth in the Federalists Papers, Declaration of Independence and our Constitution. The twin pillars of Islam and Modernity now perilously threaten it.

Adherents to Christianity, Judaism and most of the world's religions except Islam do not have violence as one of their core articles of faith.

1. Sadly, the Progressive Modernists hijacked this beautiful word and, consequently, in the 20th Century it became synonymous with their cheap, humanistic worldview.

Brian Hennessey of *Israel Today* has argued that "extremism" isn't really the problem. It is which specific religion believers are following. "[T]he more serious a moderate Muslim gets about practicing his religion, the more 'radicalized' he will become," he contended. "With those that look to the Bible, just the opposite happens. The core message of the Bible urges believers to love your neighbors as yourself, not cut their heads off. So, the more a Christian or Jew gets serious about his biblical beliefs, and practices them, the more loving and godly they become."

While it is true that only a small fraction of Islam's billion-plus of adherents are currently radicalized to the point of violence, it is equally as true that a large majority of Muslims do yearn for a world ruled by Sharia Law. This is simply incompatible with both a classically liberal Constitutional Republic and the very existence of Christianity and Judaism. Mohammed established a permanent state of war between Islam and everyone else, dividing the world into Dar al Islam and Dar al Harb (the House of War). 1,400 years of clerical decrees by the Mah'di interpreting the Hadiths and Koran (and Siyar) have done nothing to temper this world view.

How many Muslim-run states allow the free practice of other religions? How many "no-go" zones were there in many European cities such as Paris, Berlin and Malmo? The answers should be as obvious as the nose on one's face, but if a politician or commentator points these out, the Progressives immediately shout them down as being "Intolerant" or "Islamaphobic." See what England has done to Tommy Robinson. The irony of their disapprobation is the fact that Progressives will be the first to have their heads lopped off if ever the Mohammedans come to power.

In many ways Modernity is the more dangerous of the two heresies because, as does Lucifer, it mixes lies with the truth, cloaking itself in faux philosophical language and "belief" structure that virulently attacks our Founding Fathers and their sound belief structure based in faith and divine providence. In essence, Modernity denies God, or worse, mocks God and all those who express and practice their faith in Him and His natural law. Modernists also casually ignore the First Amendment, conveniently labelling any thought contrary to their dogma as "hate speech."

It has insidiously eroded the fabric of American society to the point at which now a school district in Charlotte, North Carolina[2] is considering teaching children that there are no little girls or little boys, but rather an androgynous Gender Unicorn.

2. Ironically, the National Football League and other sports groups have targeted North Carolina for boycott because of that state's law requiring people to use bathrooms based on the sex God gave them.

Had someone twenty years ago – or even ten years ago – told me that this would be discussed anywhere outside the confines of an insane asylum, I would have thought that individual balmy at best. Now, in this insane asylum of Modern America, the sane and morally upright are made to feel like inmates. And it is now time for us inmates to begin to fight back and I pray to Almighty God that many of my fellow Americans will join in this existential fight.

Modernity is that self-centric, condescending world view of most Progressives, which foolishly believes that mankind can reach paradise here on Earth via advances in science, knowledge and sheer political will. It is, distilled down to its essence, original sin: elevating man to the status of God. It is most clearly seen in its excesses like transgenderism, e.g., whereby a man rebels against the genetic code God gave him, decides to become his own God by cutting off his penis and calling himself by a girl's name. Then, not satisfied with his own self-mutilation, demands that the rest of society join in his folly. One would be just as justified in cutting off a leg, spray painting himself pink, then demanding all call him a flamingo. Sadly, that Mohammedan-Modernist mixto of a president, Barack Obama, thought it was just peachy to bring such disturbed individuals into our military. Doing so ignored not only right reason but the moral code of Christendom.

In an attack on all that is good and wholesome in America, the Progressive political machine affirms such insane acts and tries to coerce believers in the traditions of Christianity or Judaism to deny their one true God.

Some folks hear a song from their youth or smell a home-cooked meal that triggers brief flashes of their past, but my memories and recollections from different periods of my life all point to a pending doom for the Republic for which I have fought to protect for most of my adult life. Men were masculine back then and "gay" was a mood, not a euphemism for a queer. One of my friends – an F-14 Tomcat driver, call sign "Coconut" – once commented at a warfighter conference in Little Creek about the "Pussification" of America's fighting forces. "Emasculation" may be a better way of stating that truth, but American males are being turned into wimps by helicopter moms and public-school systems devoid of God and teachers like of School Sisters of Notre Dame.[3]

Everyone laughed at the time, but Coconut's

---

3. I shared the same First Grade teacher at Baltimore's Cathedral of Mary Our Queen with a much better author, George Weigel. As George so righty wrote in his brilliant book Letters to a Young Catholic, Sister Mary Moira could teach a cinder block to read. I was one of them. Even for non-Roman Catholics, I heartily commend Weigel's book. It sparkles with hidden gems from recent and distant past.

words were prophetic. How else could we have been at war with radical Islamists since 2001 and still be standing in long lines at airports and enduring multiple attacks on our home soil without even naming the enemy? The Muj – are winning because we have become spiritually and physically weak. We have lost our will while the enemy hones his hatchets. And now China and Russia (as well as Iran and North Korea) are threatening.

Now, instead of learning to be resilient, students protest to the Progressive zero-tolerance Mafiosi about micro-aggressions and grades other than an "A."

My wife, a forensic psychiatrist, often treats American soldiers with borderline personality disorders and narcissistic behavior brought about by not learning resiliency and coping skills my generation learned on the playground. The result is that many Army units are saddled with what we used to call "the sick, lame and lazy" and there is no hope on the horizon.

America and Britain defeated Nazi Germany and Imperial Japan in a third of the time we have been fiddlef*$king around with these savages. And, the Germans and Japs of World War II could really fight ... what is wrong with the West nowadays? Where are the 21st Century's version of the 8th Century's Charles Martel (Battle of Tours) or his 17th Century successor in the fight against

Mohammedans, Jan Sobieski (Siege of Vienna)? Or, even the 20th Century's Chesty Puller or Alvin York?

It astounds me that we have viable Democratic presidential candidates who are confessed socialists. "It will work if we only try harder," as university professors and the media have brainwashed dimwitted high school students, teachers, school bus drivers and millennials into believing. Hell, Hitler, Stalin, Mao and Pol Pot, as well as countless minor potentates in sub-Saharan Africa, killed over 120 million people in the 20th Century trying really hard to make it work. How many million will the Progressives send to the Gulags to make it work this time?

Think I am joking? As I write, there are divers Federal and State prosecutors scheming to imprison people for being climate change "deniers." Climate change fanatics, green parties and all of Progressivism are simply filling the vacuum left when we allowed governments to take God out of schools and our social discourse. The human soul yearns to believe in our Creator, and when society squelches that yearning, it is quite natural for man to fall into the worship of modern day Baals: drugs, doing it "My Way," climate change, animal rights, LBGTQ and all the other lies of Progressivism.

Our Founding Fathers, among them George

Washington, Charles Carroll of Carrollton, Thomas Jefferson, James Madison, Benjamin Franklin, John Adams and Patrick Henry, would shudder at what the left has done to our great republic. Also, it is oft forgotten the dispropor-tionate sacrifice of the small minority of Jews in America. In Georgia, the first patriot to be killed was a Jew, Francis Salvador. The most important of the financiers of our Revolution was Haym Salomon, who lent his fortune and then some to the Continental Congress. In the last days of the war, Salomon advanced the American govern-ment $200,000. He was never paid back and died in bankruptcy.

Contrary to the Progressive drivel that passes for a basic education in America, these men are not "dead old white men and slave owners, who could not foresee the advent of computers, airplanes, and the Internet." Rather, they were geniuses that understood the fundamental and enduring nature of mankind and wrote our Constitution as a bul-wark against that nature. Most of them spoke and wrote in two or three languages and had truly diverse interests. Now, the likes of Alexandra Ocasio-Cortez (aka "AOC") wish to destroy that document that millions of brave Americans have fought and died defending in our brief history.

The Constitution is a pact between free peoples

and their government. It confers limited powers to that government yet confers nothing to the individual. The Bill of Rights merely acknowledges what are God-given individual rights under the natural law: rights to freely associate with those we chose; the right to be armed for defense against bandits and an oppressive government; the right to be free from unfettered search and seizure; and, all the rights enumerated and more. Yet, its enforcement is critical to protecting our individual rights and limiting the powers of government. If the Modernists or Mohammedans have their way, its life will be short-lived.

These new Soviets: disinter the graves of Confederate heroes; unilaterally and without referendum take out decades-old beautiful stained glass from the National Cathedral because it "offends" the ignorant; and, plague the populace with so many laws and regulations that the average person can unknowingly commit three felonies a day.[4] I pray that we can turn our Republic around before it is too late to restore so many lost freedoms. Unless we get our own house in order and return to a community bound together by the common virtues of our Judeo-Christian monotheism, we will lose the battle with Islam and The Left. We must remain virtuous or we will be caved in by the

---

4. Silverglate, Harvey, Three Felonies a Day: How the Feds Target the Innocent, Encounter Books (2011).

true evil of Modernity that Orwell, Churchill and Chesterton warned us about. "When Man ceases to worship God, he does not worship nothing but worships everything." We must all become Saint Thomas More, a speaker of the truth no matter the cost. If not, we squander all that was given to us by our forebearers.

David G. Bolgiano, J.D., M.S.S., served in deployed locations with Special Operations Forces during Operations IRAQI FREEDOM and ENDURING FREEDOM. He also served as a paratrooper with the 82nd Airborne Division and on Faculty at the U.S. Army War College's Department of National Security & Strategy. His articles have appeared in *Proceedings*, *Wall Street Journal*, *Orbis* and diverse other magazines and law reviews. He is the author of *Combat Self-Defense*; and co-author of *Fighting Today's Wars and Virtuous Policing: Bridging America's Gulf Between Police and Populace*. Bolgiano began his career as a law enforcement officer in Baltimore.

Timeline of the Great Crusades

Judeao-Christian cultures and Islamic cultures have been at odds for almost a millennium, and there is no end in sight. Peace in the Mid-east seems to be the unattainable Holy Grail of every American President.

First Crusade (1096-99AD)
The Fall of Jerusalem (1099AD)
Second Crusade (1147-49AD)
Third Crusade (1187-92AD)
Fourth Crusade: (1202-1204AD)
Final Crusades (1208-1271AD)
The Fall of Constantinople (1453AD)

The reflection of a loved one at the Vietnam Memorial Wall.

WILLIAM C KNAUS ·
ROBERT D LEWIS
WI___UTZ · ADANO HERNENDEZ
· RODNEY H MAUNAKEA · JOSEPH E
MICHAEL J MITCHELL · WAVERY MOO
· JOSEPH P McKNIGHT
· MICHAEL S O'BRIEN · TIMOTH
· RAYMOND F NORVELL · MARVIN E
· MARION D POWELL · A
· ROBERT A ROOSSIEN · C
· ARTHUR E SCOTT · RONALD M SETTIM
· NATHAN B SIMMONS · OLEN
· JAMES V SPURLEY Jr · EDSEL W STEA
· ISAIAH T STUKES · CHARLES
· CHARLES THOMAS Jr · CARL THO
· BERTALAN J TOTH · ESTEBAN A TREVIN
· ALBERTO RIOS VASQUEZ J
· WENDELL A WESTON · THOMAS A WH
· ROGER E WOOSTER ·
· SCOTT F ANDRESEN · CARL F ARE
+ BRUCE C BESSOR · P
· JERRY C BOCK · KILB
· GALEN C BROWN · DAVID F BUKO
· KENNETH T CRUISE Jr · MARTIN L DAN
· JAMES R DUNKLE · JAME
· THOMAS E FOSTER · MOULTON L B

Fake news can broadly be defined as false information. It is comprised of information designed to mislead readers/listeners/viewers, for either social, political, or financial gain.

CHAPTER 17

MEDIA LIES

BY BOB BECKER

FREEDOM WOULD BE A much more inspiring word if it wasn't open to interpretation.

Among several tries, the dictionary says it is "Liberty of choice or action," and that has never been more evident than it is today.

In more respectful days, freedom meant that you could do or say what you wanted to, provided you didn't lie, deceive or cause harm.

Why? Because it was the right way to act, and at one time that actually mattered. That is no longer the case. Back "then" you could try to get away with lies, deception or harmful behavior, but if you got caught, reparations would be swift and harsh. Not anymore.

Walk down the street wearing the wrong colors, and you are liable to be accosted, screamed at, punched or kicked. Represent the wrong political party, and your family might be chased out of a restaurant or a movie theater.

THE EXAMPLES ARE TOO MANY TO LIST.

Trying to speak in public, or invite a speaker who agrees with you, but not "them," might cause a mini-riot, not to mention bodily harm.

And that is why Freedom of the Press has been eroded so badly, with barely a whimper of protest.

A press cannot truly be free unless it is fair. To be otherwise is to be completely owned by an ideology that puts dogma ahead of truth, partisanship ahead of honesty, persecution ahead of professionalism.

Where there once was truth, today there is hatred. Where there once was professional pride, we now have anger. Where once it mattered to be right, beyond anything else, today the most important thing is to be on the right side, and present the right slant.

If the other side does good, it is imperative to tear the accomplishment down, even if the only way to do that is with a lie or using an "anonymous" source to simply make up a story.

Last year three Texas researchers completed a study that said violence increased by 226 percent in areas where President Trump had just given a speech. The media jumped all over it.

Then three Harvard researchers did a peer review of the study and proved it was faulty, that the math was way off base. Using the same math the Texas group had used, the Harvard group showed that violence exploded even more in areas after Hillary Clinton spoke.

Using the correct math, they showed virtually no spike in violence no matter who had talked.

The media headlined the Trump accusation for days, yet never mentioned the later Clinton assessment. And when Harvard completely disproved the Texas study, nobody offered a correction, and virtually nobody mentioned it.

That was just one in a long line of media deceptions.

Not that long ago, MSNBC anchor Lawrence O'Donnell went on the air to breathlessly share a scoop. He said he had information that Donald Trump had called on Russian oligarchs with close ties to Vladimir Putin for loans to help build a Moscow hotel.

On air, O'Donnell said he had not seen the signed documents himself, and later said his anonymous source had not seen them either. But he went with the story anyway, and it was immediately picked up by many other media outlets.

How did that story get airtime? Where were the editors and producers? He admitted he had one source who told him he hadn't actually seen the documents. And the other media outlets that ran with the story knew that he had not seen any supporting evidence, and neither had his source.

But it was just too juicy to pass up. O'Donnell apologized the next day, and withdrew the story. But the damage had been done. To today's media, a lie often has more value than truth.

The press has always been defined by its leanings. Whatever town you grew up in had either a conservative or liberal newspaper, and the editorial page would excoriate the Democrats or Republicans, depending on which way they leaned. And it didn't take long for you to figure out which side your TV station supported. But that was OK, because for the most part, the news coverage was straight. No editorializing, just simple reporting: Who What, Where, Why and When. Journalism 101. Anonymous sources were rarely used, and then only after multiple levels of scrutiny.

Unfortunately, today we don't just see slanted news. We see outright lies. And worse, the lies are accepted so long as they take the proper side.

We just finished two years, and millions of

dollars, spent on the so-called "Russian election investigation".

It was a hoax, perpetrated, orchestrated and paid for by one party. Not only did the hoax fail, the investigation by a special counsel blew it out of the water.

TELEVISION IS JUST AS GUILTY.

There are a lot of anchors on TV. They are filled with the same zeal to harm the other side as newspaper writers.

MSNBC's Nicole Wallace recently said on the air that President Trump wanted to "exterminate Latinos."

Univision's Jorge Ramos once said on the air that President Trump had said Mexicans were rapists and criminals. That was a lie. One of the biggest lies was the tumult after Trump said there were some fine people at the march in Charlottesville. It was a march to call attention to the destruction of Confederate statues.

Antifa and white supremacists clashed at the march, but they weren't the only ones marching. Churches had representation, as well as civic and historical groups. They all got caught up, and quickly moved away, from the conflict.

But even today you still hear that Trump had said that some Nazis were fine people. A complete lie repeated over and over again on television and in print.

What he said was there were some fine people at the march … and there were.

During the border crisis, President Trump talked about the "invasion" of illegal aliens. He was criticized across the country on TV and in newspapers for using the term invasion, which was a word deemed "racist."

Somebody forgot that Article 4, Section 4 of the Constitution says that we "shall protect the Nation from invasion."

This is an industry that has a proven 92 percent rate of negative coverage against the current administration. That is one of the big reasons only politicians and used car salesmen rate lower on national respect polls.

Despite more people working today than in the history of the country, despite the lowest unemployment for African Americans, Hispanics and women, despite a huge jump in the Gross Domestic Product, despite large increases in manufacturing jobs returning to the United States, despite energy independence and despite eight million fewer Americans depending on food stamps, more than nine of 10 news stories day after day are negative in nature.

HOW TO EXPLAIN WHAT IS GOING ON?

One of the loudest voices in Congress these

days is Representative Alexandra Ocasio Cortez (D-New York).

She recently defined the current thinking.

"I think there's a lot of people more concerned about being precisely, factually and semantically correct," she said, "than about being morally right."

And she was being dead serious.

For close to 250 years, millions of young American men and women have stepped forward, taken the oath and gone off to defend our country and our Constitution.

More than a million paid the ultimate price, and today we still have thousands standing guard for the rest of us.

But too many of our citizens...and politicians...forget that with our inalienable rights comes responsibility. Our country was founded on working for the common good, doing things or making decisions simply because those are the right things to do, and will benefit us as a nation.

A military unit will not survive if there is divisiveness in the ranks. Neither will a country.

The Bill of Rights is the backbone of our Constitution and our country. It offers guidance, order and protection. But responsibility must go hand in hand with the rights themselves. Right now one side of the political spectrum is being pilloried. Proponents of the other side need to remember that these things go in cycles, and if things don't return to the way they should be, their turn is yet to come.

Freedom of the Press will not matter if the people decide the press is not honest or trustworthy. We should be able to believe what we are told or read, but today the majority of the American public does not.

And for good reason.

For centuries the military has stood together... black, white, Hispanic, Catholic, Jewish, Baptist, Methodist, Republican, Democrat, vegan...all sections of America...to keep our nation strong and free.

"We leave no one behind" is our mantra.

That concept is so foreign to today's society that it is anybody's guess where the country is headed.

Press freedom should enhance our lives, because an informed society is a strong, united society.

Lies, half truths, misinformation and misdirection benefits only the small few who chose domination over democracy.

Too many American heroes gave up their lives to guarantee press freedom. Too many unworthy egos have turned the concept inside out.

It was just a short time ago that the New York Times published...to enough fanfare that

Democrat presidential candidates immediately began a clamor for impeachment...a story claiming sexual misconduct from Supreme Court Justice Brett Cavanaugh.

The Times left out the fact that the reporters had never talked to the supposed victim, who had repeatedly denied in the past any knowledge of the event. Then they quoted a "witness" a former lawyer for Bill Clinton...who they also never interviewed. What the reporters used was information from the lawyer's friends who said they heard him make that statement.

"This attempt is beyond disgusting and speaks to the dishonesty of leading organs of the mainstream media, " said Fox News Brit Hume. "They are corrupt."

The Solution

The solution is to think critically, not irrationally. When reading an article, ask yourself one major question: "why has this article been written or story been reported?" If you can think it could be trying to persuade you of an individual viewpoint or is acting as a marketing ploy to purchase a product, then it's likely that the news is fake.

Not only can articles allude you from the truth, but counterfeit images can also take on the same role. While we have moved mountains in the technological world to make content more accessible, modern editing software has made it easy for fake images to be created. Often these images look professional and real, and recent research has revealed that only half of the people viewing them can identify whether they are fake or not.

Finally, over the past 15 years I've taught at a local college; I've had a good number of combat veterans from the Gulf Wars. All reported that upon returning from a mission they would often see that action reported on TV; they said that Fox News got the reports right about half the time—no other network ever got it right. CNN was called by them the Communist News Network, because they never heard anything good about America on that channel.

We, the people, need to communicate with our media and let them know that we want accurate reporting—all the time.

Bob Becker is a former Air Force staff sergeant who spent 45 years in newspapers. His professional experience includes reporting beats on cops and courts, state government and education, and he has been a city editor, news editor and sports editor. In retirement he spent seven years as an adjunct professor of journalism at the university level. He has spent the last 13 years as a member of his county veterans honor guard, taking part in some 1,200 military funerals. He is a past honor guard commander and also county Veteran of the Year.

The White House, located at 1600 Pennsylvania Ave in Washington DC, has been the residence of every US President since John Adams in 1800. More importantly, it is the symbol of the Executive branch of government, established by the US Constitution.

As a rule hate is the outcome of fear. It is human nature to fear what you don't understand.

CHAPTER 18

I HATE HATE

BY DENNY GILLEM

THERE IS ONE THING I REally hate—that's hatred. Hatred is most commonly expressed by namecalling—to be specific, names or descriptions that are totally inaccurate, belittling, and lacking any evidence except the proclamation of the hater. You may or may not have noticed that there is quite a bit of that happening on the political scene; it's been acute since Donald Trump won the Republican nomination.

I've run for office a couple of times and, during those campaigns I was occasionally called names. Trust me, I blew off the names, especially when

I considered who was calling me the names. But my family was hurt by the names I was called. I stopped running for office so that they would stop being hurt.

For the first time that I can remember, the name-callers are not only targeting the candidate or office holder—in this case, President Trump, but they're also targeting his wife and young son—not to mention his older children. One must truly be full of and ruled by hate to do such things—in my opinion.

I find it really interesting that the president is regularly called a racist when he has lowered Black unemployment to the lowest level since records were kept. Black businesses have skyrocketed—over 400%. Wages for Black workers have gone up. He signed a Prison reform bill and has pardoned wrongfully convicted people of color—all of which none of his predecessors have done, and none of the people calling him a racist have even come close to doing. And they have zero examples of him ever espousing anything racist.

I suspect that this sounds like I'm trying to praise and promote the president—but what I'm trying to do is show how wildly incorrect are the names he's being called—the sign of hatred—and also how the media doesn't point out these lies—another sign of hatred.

American Military Veterans

Think about this. If I were a candidate or office holder and you heard me say that in my opinion my race was superior to another race—and I meant it—would you call me a racist? Probably not, because that's a term used commonly against people, and it normally lacks any evidence. No, you would probably state the fact that you heard me say that my race was superior. That's not name-calling; that's fact reporting. It's not hate-based; it's clearly stated fact-based.

As a general rule, when a person who lacks character really dislikes another and is lacking in facts, they attack the humanity of their opponent—by name-calling. One's humanity is attacked by calling the opponent a liar, a racist, a homophobe, a bigot, and on and on. And there is no way to refute these things—because it's impossible to prove a negative.

Now, to some extent, there will always be some minor name-calling during a heated campaign. It's not good, but it just happens. We can't always fully control what comes out of our mouths when emotions are flowing. That's not to excuse name-calling, but we must recognize that none of us are perfect.

This might be my personal bias showing, but I have a bit more understanding for our president since he's had hundreds and hundreds of prominent people on the political left attacking not only his humanity, but also that of his wife and children. I'm not sure how long I could tolerate that evil, unreasonable, un-Godly flow without striking back.

So, where am I going with this? Let's set a goal for this year of being intolerant of name-calling, of attacks on any person's humanity. Let your elected officials and candidates know that you personally find such conduct both unworthy and beneath contempt—and that you won't put up with it.

There is absolutely nothing wrong with disliking a person or official or totally disagreeing with the position someone takes on some issue. It's fine to proclaim that you dislike and don't support an office-holder or candidate or that you'll oppose anyone who votes for or against an issue you care about. But don't attack their humanity.

It's my observation that most name-callers are describing themselves when they throw out evil names. I suspect that they know and are not proud of themselves, so they justify themselves by accusing others of being racists or liars or stupid or whatever.

If two people disagree on an issue, they can argue the pro's and con's of the issue for hours, months, or years—and still be friends. But the minute you attack a person's humanity—much less that of their family—don't ever expect them to want to cooperate with you on anything.

We need an America where we can disagree without being hateful. We should proclaim that people who regularly and viciously attack the humanity of others are basically evil people who need to repent.

The strength of America is our diversity, but we diverse people must be able to work together. Let's all hate HATE.

Lieutenant Colonel Dennis J. Gillem is a 1964 graduate of the United States Military Academy at West Point, and a Vietnam combat veteran. He served two tours in Vietnam as a company grade officer where he received seven US awards for valor. After a distinguished military career he retired and now lives in Michigan with his wife and is an Adjunct Professor of Political Science.

LTC Gillem hosts the nationally syndicated military talk radio show, *Frontlines of Freedom*, which is heard every weekend nation-wide. Go to www.frontlinesoffreedom.com for local station listings and for podcasts.

The Solution

Our nation is somehow full of hate. I've been politically active since I retired from the Army in 1986. There have been candidates that I joyously supported and others that I worked hard against. But I never hated any of them. Many did things I thought were inappropriate, wrong, and sometimes criminal—but I never hated them—nor did my friends. I was unaware of any hatred in any of my opponents, either.

As a rule hate is the outcome of fear. I believe the reason there is so much hate in the political arena today is that many of the prominent politicians on all sides of the spectrum see their empires falling. (I call their empires the Swamp.) President Trump is keeping his campaign promises and has made our nation's economy—and especially our unemployment rate—the best in generations. And he's doing it without using the "experts" in the swamp—those are the career politicians and civil servants who have always had power—regardless of who was president.

These Swamp-rats fear the permanent loss of their power—thus they exude hate—and it's the reason for their lies and non-stop searching for dirt. (But not their own dirt.)

Let's not put up with hate. If someone exudes hate towards anyone—ask them why; don't accept non-specific answers. Ask them how it feels to live with hate.

Let's all Hate HATE

Our nation's national debt is the total debt, or unpaid borrowed funds, carried by the federal government. Government debt increases as a result of government spending, and decreases from tax or other receipts. As of February 2020, the total national debt was $23.25 trillion. This debt has more than doubled in the last ten years. Our grandchildren are going to have to pay it off—or our nation could go broke—that's what happened to the Soviet Union.

Given this, why would we not want to secure our borders so that we can use our funds to take care of American citizens—especially veterans. Why would we not want to repair our worn-out roads and utilities? Why would we not want to control who comes into our nation so that we don't suddenly find ourselves spending more money—money that we don't have—supporting people who are not contributing in any way to our nation? We need to secure our border, now!

CHAPTER 19

OPPOSITION TO ILLEGAL IMMIGRATION VOICED BY THE LEADERS OF THE DEMOCRAT PARTY

BY CAPT JOSEPH R. JOHN

THE UNITED STATES WEL-comes over 1 million legal immi-grants to the United States from foreign countries each year who follow certain applicant procedures to identify themselves. No other country in the world has ever welcomed over 1 million Legal Immigrants to their country each year.

Every Democrat Party leader over the last 40 years expressed their opposition to illegal immigration except for Nancy Pelosi, who is a proponent for Open Borders, and promotes the entry of illegal aliens.

We recommend you share this message with those in your address book who oppose the entry each week of over 15,000 illegal aliens from 23 countries, who are now invading the United States through the wide open southern border. They are now entering in organized migrant caravans; even as I write these words, there is a 12,000 migrant caravan currently en route to the United States. The organizers are aware that the Democrats in Congress are preventing President Trump from securing the wide open southern border.

Entrants include MS 13 gang members, drug smugglers, radical Islamic terrorists, human traffickers, convicted criminal illegal aliens who were released from US prisons, and the scourge of opioids which are killing 194,500 mostly young Americans each day. More Americans are dying each day from opioids than are dying each day from breast cancer.

The migrant caravan invasions (of mostly men) in November and December 2018 were not spontaneous, they were highly organized; their goal was to "degrade US Security." They were organized by multiple UN Agencies, numerous "Open Borders" organizations, CAIR, MECHA, the American Friends Services Committee (a

Quaker group that has had ties to the Communist Party since the 1920s), and Chicago-based organizations founded by Left Wing Activists, Emma Lozano-Pueblo Sin Fronteras, La Familia Latino Unida, and Centro Sin Fronteras Community Services Network.

The migrant caravan invasions in November and December 2018 had 100 Pueblo Sin Fronteras workers embedded with the caravans. "Open Borders" organizations and philanthropists covered the cost of chartered bus transportation, food for thousands of illegal aliens. Those providing funding included George Soros, the International Association of Democratic Lawyers (a Soviet Propaganda Front), National Lawyer Guild (a Communist front), Casa de Maryland (Communist Open Borders front), The Ford Foundation (which funds Leftists and Communist organizations), Illinois Dept. of Human Services, Catholic Legal Immigration Network, Refugee Rights, National Immigration Forum, etc.

The illegal aliens are entering the United States in violation of US Federal Immigration Quarantine Laws, that at one time were enforced, requiring 90-day quarantines of immigrants who Public Health Doctors suspected had communicable diseases. If they determined any immigrants had a communicable disease, and that there would be a danger of spreading it to the general population, that immigrant was returned to their country of origin.

The Center For Disease Control and Prevention (CDC) cautioned that Americans are now being exposed to highly contagious disease that had previously been eradicated, because over 15,000 illegal aliens entering the US each week, are no longer being quarantined to detect communicable diseases. The infections of illegal aliens is responsible for the reemergence of small pox, mumps, polio, tuberculosis, lice, leprosy, scabies, diphtheria, staph infections, etc. that are now being detected in the general population. Illegal aliens are infecting both US Border Patrol Agents who have contact with them, and grammar school children, in public schools, who are required to be in class with the children of illegal aliens, who for the most part cannot even speak English.

The US House of Representatives and the US Senate have the solemn obligation to protect American Citizens from the out-of-control invasion entering the US across the wide-open southern border, especially by Radical Islamic Terrorists, drug smugglers, criminal-convicted illegal aliens, MS-13 gang members, and human traffickers who regularly rape the young girls and women they are bringing into the United States each week.

American Military Veterans

In November 2018, 62,000 illegal aliens were interdicted coming across the wide open southern border, and in December 2018, over 70,000 illegal aliens were interdicted coming across the wide open southern border, a 78 percent increase over the same period last year; and most likely, two-thirds that number each month were not interdicted, and entered illegally.

The United States has a broken US Immigration System. Only the US Congress can pass legislation to fix it. President Trump cannot fix it. The Combat Veterans For Congress PAC will recruit a new slate of conservative combat veterans to run and be elected in 2020 with your help, in order to join the 17 endorsed and elected Combat Veterans For Congress, who will mobilize support to fix the broken US Immigration System.

Joseph R. John retired from the US Navy at the rank of Captain. He is a graduate of the United States Naval Academy, class of 1962. He also served in the FBI as a Counter Terrorist Intelligence Analyst. He was also deployed to Kuwait with Special Operations Command Central during Operation Desert Storm.

Joe John is now serving as the Chairman and Director of Combat Veterans For Congress PAC, which was founded in August 2009 to rein in the out of control spending by an irresponsible Congress.

Something to Consider

I would not be happy if a stranger walked into my home, sat down, and waited for me to feed him and give him a place to live. If I want my home secure from un-invited guests, why should I not feel that way about my nation? We need to decide who may enter our nation and how long they may stay. We should not welcome anyone who won't contribute to making ours a better nation. Yes, we can take in a few people who are being seriously abused by their home nation, but we are, first and foremost, the home for our citizens.

We need to have all of our borders secure—and the most violated one, by far, is our border with Mexico. We need to build the wall—now!

The US Capitol building was
originally completed in 1800.
It was partially burned by
the British during the War of
1812 on August 24, 1814.
Reconstruction began in 1815.

January 30, 1835 - On this date, Richard
Lawrence, an unemployed and insane
housepainter from England made the first-
ever attempt to kill a sitting President of
the United States. At the time, President
Andrew Jackson was exiting the East
Portico after the funeral of South Carolina
Representative Warren Davis. The assassin stepped out from behind a column
and aimed a pistol at Jackson, but the gun
misfired. Lawrence pulled another gun but
it also misfired. President Jackson then
attacked the assassin with a cane until he
was taken into custody.

Our nation's national debt is the total debt, or unpaid borrowed funds, carried by the federal government. Government debt increases as a result of government spending, and decreases from tax or other receipts. As of February 2020, the total national debt was $23.25 trillion. This debt has more than doubled in the last ten years. Our grandchildren are going to have to pay it off—or our nation could go broke—that's what happened to the Soviet Union.

Given this, why would we not want to secure our borders so that we can use our funds to take care of American citizens—especially veterans. Why would we not want to repair our worn-out roads and utilities? Why would we not want to control who comes into our nation so that we don't suddenly find ourselves spending more money—money that we don't have—supporting people who are not contributing in any way to our nation? We need to secure our border, now!

CHAPTER 20

THE EFFECTS OF TECHNOLOGY ON OUR CULTURE

BY CHRIS KOHLMEIR

WE ARE LIVING IN A TIME of more interconnectedness than ever before. Information is available at our fingertips within an instant. We interact with people from all over the world digitally, and in real time. We are experiencing a technological explosion that has spread extremely rapidly over the past 10 years. Technology, social media, cell phones especially—have taken a foothold within our society almost overnight. The broad reach and influence of social media and other "insta-communication" platforms are nothing short of amazing. The level of interconnectedness is something we have only begun experiencing as a society, and it comes with great responsibility. Interconnectedness can be a great tool for good but the long-term effects of this technology and mass-communication on society are not yet apparent to us and must be carefully observed. The potential for technology to improve our society is exciting but we must remain diligent because frankly, we are in uncharted territory.

Alongside the potential good, there are downsides. If we are not careful, if we do not take the time to teach our young how to navigate a righteous path in this life, they will absorb information elsewhere. They may absorb information misaligned with the traditional values that have made our country so great to begin with. Dr. Martin Luther King Jr. summarized it best, "If we are not careful, our colleges will produce a group of close-minded, unscientific, illogical propagandists, consumed with immoral acts. Be careful, 'brethren! ' Be careful, teachers". We must actively choose what to teach our young people, or it will be chosen for us.

Social media isn't as social as we think. People are actively avoiding short-term, temporarily uncomfortable experiences required to build and develop strong character values. Handling rejection, overcoming failure, adapting to adversity—

all critical prerequisites for success— are lessons lost the longer we continue hide behind screens. Many people in our country are shifting toward a "coddle culture" and it has become quite apparent with the countless new excuses "explaining" this or that, pointing out why there is a lack in equality of outcome in their lives. We must not confuse equal opportunity with equality of outcome.

Our society is developing an issue with the ability to handle criticism. Young people are having trouble dealing with conflict. Handling conflict is what helps us grow. If avoided, we merely compartmentalize problems and create division instead of coming together to collaborate to create the best ideas to benefit this great nation. Society is shifting further and further away from the very foundations that hold us together. The path needs to be corrected. Community, togetherness, unity—these are becoming more and more distant as technology brings us "closer together". It is time we put some serious thought into how much time we allow ourselves to be exposed to information technology.

Even with the readily available information about health, fitness, and general wellness and yet we have the highest rates of obesity our country has ever seen. The National Center for Health Statistics estimates that, for 2015-2016 in the U.S., 39.8% of adults aged 20 and over were obese (including 7.6% with severe obesity) and that another 31.8% were overweight. Obesity rates have increased for all population groups in the United States over the last few decades. Screen time negatively correlates with our physical health, and it is common knowledge that phone apps are psychologically addicting. We are witnessing anxiety, depression and suicides climbing while we ignorantly stare into the bright blue abyss of our screens.

Technology and information systems are not going away. These will ultimately be the catalysts for improving the lives of people or they will be the great distractors pulling attention away from the truly important things. We need to pay special attention to the inherent dangers these platforms provide and strive to strike a balance with what we expose ourselves to if we are to preserve the culture upon which our great nation was founded.

Chris Kohlmeir is a dedicated, action-oriented professional leader who possesses a wide range of operational experience, including logistics, inventory management, and communications management. He spent four years in the Marine Corps as a Command and Control officer aboard Camp Lejeune, NC. He deployed to Norway in support of Operation Cold Response in 2015-2016 as the Combat Logistics Battalion 252 Combat Operations Center Officer. After returning to the United States he finished his active service and worked as an inventory control manager for Nike, and later a project manager for Schindler Elevator Corporation. Chris left his job in June of 2019 to pursue an MBA full time. He currently works as a Congressional Campaign Manager for Alan Hoover 2020 in Michigan's 8th District.

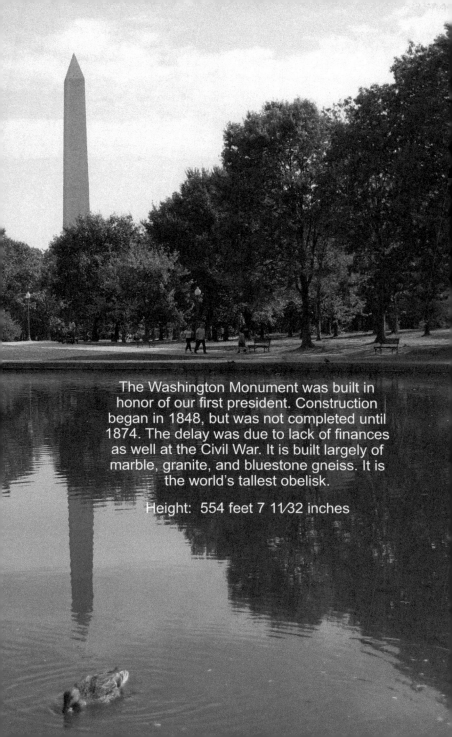

The Washington Monument was built in honor of our first president. Construction began in 1848, but was not completed until 1874. The delay was due to lack of finances as well at the Civil War. It is built largely of marble, granite, and bluestone gneiss. It is the world's tallest obelisk.

Height: 554 feet 7 11/32 inches

"We also know from science that the unborn baby has a completely different set of DNA from the mother and father, 23 chromosomes coming from the father and 23 from the mother. At fertilization they combine into 46 chromosomes and a new human being is formed. The heart begins beating at three weeks and by the third month the developing fetus looks like a tiny human being. Clearly it is not part of the mother's body. It is a separate entity, a separate human being fully deserving of life."

CHAPTER 21

A CULTURE OF DEATH

BY PAT MORAN

AMERICA HAS FALLEN INTO an abyss of tyranny where the majority allows and indeed celebrates the right to kill the most innocent of all human beings: the unborn. Since abortion was legalized in 1973 by the Supreme Court in the Roe vs Wade decision, 60,942,033 unborn children have been eliminated, denied the right to life, all in the name of "choice". America has lost its moral foundation, elevating self over God, if they even acknowledge there is a God. Abortion has become the central galvanizing issue for the Democratic party in every election, especially in presidential elections, because the sitting president gets to nominate judges to the Supreme Court. The Court has been the holy grail for Democrats and liberals since 1973, and now with the liberal majority threatened by the appointment of Justice Kavanaugh, the battle has also moved to the statehouses. Meanwhile, many Americans slumber while the abortion mills turn out their daily grisly business, which is conveniently "out of sight, out of mind". This is the great moral issue of our time. It remains to be seen if our country will wake up in time to stay the hand of judgment from Almighty God, who must certainly be grieving the slaughtering of His precious children.

Abortion is defined as "the termination of a pregnancy after, accompanied by, resulting in, or closely followed by the death of the embryo or fetus: such as: a. miscarriage and b. induced expulsion of a human fetus."[1]. The Center for Disease Control (CDC) reports in 2015 (the latest year they have reported) that 638,169 legal induced abortions were performed. That comes to 118 abortions per 1000 women 15-44 years old and 188 abortions per 1000 live births.[2] A more

1-Merriam-Webster.com
2-MMWR: Abortion Surveillance- United States, 2015

recent statistic from The US Abortion Clock.org web site says there have been a total of 732,968 abortions performed from January 1st through Oct 15, 2019, of which 7109 were from rape or incest (.96% of all abortions)[3] What do Americans think of this carnage? In a survey by The Pew Research Center, 63% of Americans don't want to see abortion overturned, while 29% want it eliminated. This result has stayed consistent for the past 20 years.[4] In another startling statistic, only 62% of Americans know Roe vs Wade is about abortion, and for those under 30 years old, only 44% know that Roe vs Wade is about abortion.[5]How has America gotten to this point where abortion on demand is the law of the land?

From 1850-1900, nearly all states banned abortions throughout pregnancy, although some allowed exceptions when a woman's life was in danger. Between 1962-1973, 17 states passed laws to allow abortions for health risks, rape, and fetal damage.[6]But the general law of the land did not allow abortions. Then along came Jane Roe in 1973, who challenged the Texas criminal abortion laws that banned abortions except on medical advice for the purpose of saving the mother's life.

3-US Abortion Clock.org
4-Pew Research Center
5 IBID
6-IBID

Justice Blackmun delivered the majority opinion in a 7-2 decision, and although abortion in the first trimester was allowed without restriction, the second and third trimester abortions could be regulated according to the "compelling interest" of the state. However, further court cases (particularly Doe vs Bolton) allowed abortions for the "health" of the mother, which included all factors: physical, emotional, psychological, familial, and the woman's age. Or in other words, an abortion could be performed for whatever reason the mother deemed appropriate, at any stage of pregnancy. This was now a right guaranteed by the constitution under a "right of privacy", which ironically is nowhere to be found in the constitution. What reasons exactly did the "health of the mother" entail?

Let's take a look at some of the reasons why the State could not regulate abortions by looking at the words penned by Justice Blackmun himself in his majority opinion of Roe v Wade:

> *"This right of privacy, whether it be founded in the Fourteenth Amendment's concept of personal liberty and restrictions upon state action, as we feel it is, or, as the District Court determined, in the Ninth Amendment's reservation of rights to the people, is broad enough to encompass a woman's*

decision whether or not to terminate her pregnancy. The detriment that the State would impose upon the pregnant woman by denying this choice altogether is apparent. Specific and direct harm medically diagnosable even in early pregnancy may be involved. Maternity, or additional offspring, may force upon the woman a distressful life and future. Psychological harm may be imminent. Mental and physical health may be taxed by child care. There is also the distress, for all concerned, associated with the unwanted child, and there is the problem of bringing a child into a family already unable, psychologically and otherwise, to care for it. In other cases, as in this one, the additional difficulties and continuing stigma of unwed motherhood may be involved. All these are factors the woman and her responsible physician necessarily will consider in consultation. "[7]

The killing factories churned out abortions ever since, for whatever reason the mother chose. Abortion became a huge money maker, particularly for Planned Parenthood, the largest provider of abortions in the United States. They performed

7-Supreme Court decision Roe v Wade

321,384 abortions in 2016, according to their 2016-2017 annual report, netting them $1.4 billion in revenue in Fiscal Year 2017.[8] The debate has intensified every year since 1973, with various states trying to place incremental restrictions on abortions and liberal organizations promptly filing lawsuits. Liberal states have tried to do the opposite by enshrining the right to abortion in state law. New York, on the 46th anniversary of Roe v Wade, passed "The Reproductive Health Act", a law allowing abortions up to the moment of birth. The signing ceremony was celebrated by clapping and cheering politicians. Governor Cuomo made it clear the bill was a hedge against a possible Supreme Court Ruling striking down Roe vs Wade, and called it "an historic victory for New Yorkers and for our progressive values". He lit up New York skyscrapers in pink and said it was "to celebrate this achievement and shine a bright light forward for the rest of the nation to follow".[9]He wants to put the bill into the state constitution so it can never be changed. State Senator Liz Krueger stated: "the decision about whether to have an abortion is deeply personal and the government should not play a role in that

8-Lifenews.com: Planned Parenthood's Own State Show it Does More Abortions, Less Women's Health Care, Sep 14, 2018
9-Reproductive Health Act Jan 23, 2019, Fox News

decision."[10]The Virginia legislature is considering a bill that the governor indicated would allow
the physician to kill the baby AFTER birth if it
had certain abnormalities. A brilliant plan from
the pro-abortionists was to hi-jack the verbiage
to their advantage, calling abortion a "woman's
choice". Who isn't for choice in America? But in
this case they don't advertise the "choice" stands
for either killing a fetus or letting it live. The media got into the act by labeling all Pro-Lifers as
"anti-abortionists". Doesn't everyone prefer to
be "for" something rather than "anti" something?
Plus, calling someone "pro-life" assumes the fetus
is a living being, which cannot be allowed if the
abortion industry is to continue unabated. What
changed in the culture in the years leading up to
1973 and afterwards?

Feminism and the sexual revolution played an
important role in changes to the abortion laws in
the states. Women wanted control over their bodies and they wanted consequence-free sex. It was
recreational and they had a backup plan if they
happened to get pregnant. This started manifest-
ing itself in the 1960's, and the primary impetus
behind it was the decoupling of society from
the moral values found in the Bible. This trend
started with the banning of prayer from the public
schools, and has accelerated right up to the present

10-Fox News Jan 23, 2019

day. Removing of the Ten Commandments from our courthouses and other public places, rulings that crucifixes on public property are an unconstitutional establishment of religion, censoring students' speeches at graduation ceremonies, rulings legalizing same sex marriage, granting of more and more rights to the LGBTQ community, essentially legitimatizing that lifestyle, to name just a few of the cultural norms that have changed over the last 50 years. President Obama stated in his book, *The Audacity of Hope*, that "whatever we used to be, we are no longer a Christian nation".[11]He is probably right on that point, as most Christian norms have been torn down. Christians have been shamed into keeping their beliefs to themselves and not expressing their faith in the public arena. But what happens when a country separates itself from the Bible and its moral codes?

Let's first take a look at what some of our founding fathers had to say about government and religion:

> *"Laws without morals are in vain".*
> *– Benjamin Franklin*

> *"Our constitution was made only for a moral and religious people".*
> *– John Adams*

11-The Audacity of Hope, Barak Obama

*"Of all the dispositions and habits
which lead to political prosperity,
religion and morality are indispensable
supports. In vain would that man claim
tribute to patriotism who should labor
to subvert these great pillars of human
happiness —these firmest props of the
duties of men and citizens… reason
and experience both forbid us to expect
that national morality can prevail in
exclusion of religious principles."*
— *George Washington*[12]

Similarly, the Declaration of Independence declares the nation's adherence to God and His principles:

*"We hold these truths to be self-evident,
that all men are created equal, that
they are endowed by their Creator with
certain unalienable rights, that among
these are life, liberty and the pursuit of
happiness."*

We can see how important religion and moral values were to our founding fathers and to the proper functioning of our democracy. Indeed <u>they say we are</u> in great peril if we forget God

12-AZ Quotes: George Washington, John Adams, Benjamin Franklin

and religion, which is what we are currently doing in this country. The key issue today is: whose morals and values will guide this country ... man's or God's? If we reject God's, then we also reject absolute truth. The country is cast adrift morally, and no one can argue against anything the majority or the ones in power deem to be acceptable. Thus we see the abortion industry flourishing for over 40 years, and the Pro-Life movement having little effect on stopping it. Nine unelected judges deemed it acceptable (and constitutional), with Justice Blackmun stating in his majority opinion: "we need not decide when life begins". Indeed, without God and a higher moral authority, man can decide what is right and wrong and who are we to argue? But that is exactly the point today. There IS a God and He has a written moral code in the Bible. We do have to decide when life begins, because everyone in this country has a right to life. It is self-evident ... if you believe in God. He endows this right, it is unalienable, which means "not capable of being taken away or denied".[13]There is no debate if we take God at His Word and examine what the Bible has to say about the humanity of the unborn. Genesis 1:27 (NIV) says:

"So God created mankind in his own

13-Merriam Webster online dictionary

*image, in the image of God he created
them; male and female he created
them."*

Psalm 139:13 (NIV) says:
*"For you created my inmost being;
you knit me together in my mother's
womb."*

and further in verse 16 (NIV):
*"Your eyes saw my unformed body;
all the days ordained for me were
written in your book before one of them
came to be."*

In the book of Jeremiah, we see that God not only formed him in the womb, He knew him even BEFORE he was formed in the womb. Jeremiah 1:5 (NIV) says:

*"Before I formed you in the womb I
knew you, before you were born I set
you apart; I appointed you as a prophet
to the nations."*

Clearly God testifies to the humanity of the unborn from the moment of conception. We also know from science that the unborn baby has a completely different set of DNA from the mother and father, 23 chromosomes coming from the father and 23 from the mother. At fertilization they combine into 46 chromosomes and a new human being is formed. The heart begins beating at three weeks and by the third month the developing fetus looks like a tiny human being. Clearly it is not part of the mother's body. It is a separate entity, a separate human being fully deserving of life. It is totally defenseless. To kill it before birth is immoral and against God's law. Yet we as a society tolerate this tragedy in the name of "choice", or we simply look the other way.

The consequences of abortion are immense. It devalues life. If we can kill an innocent defenseless baby, what's to keep us from killing the aged or infirm, or a baby born with a birth defect, as the Virginia law would have us do? If we are not born in the image of God, what would stop an individual from a mass shooting or leaving a backpack bomb at the end of a marathon? And we wonder how someone can be so sick as to fire on a crowd from the window of a hotel, or walk into a church and randomly kill those engaged in prayer or worship. While the motivations of a mass killer are no doubt complex, a rejection of God in our society certainly plays a role. These are merely symptoms of a society without God, where life is cheap and has no real meaning. We are not guided by or are responsible to a higher authority. We are left with a chilling reality today that was also true in the time of the Judges.

> *"In those days Israel had no king;*
> *everyone did as they saw fit."*
> *Judges 21:25 (NIV)*

To reverse the culture of death, we must first return to God in our personal lives. We must recognize Jesus Christ as our Lord and Savior, teach Biblical truths to our children and bring God and the Bible back into our schools. In the political realm, Americans need to vote for Pro-Life politicians who will stand for the right to life of the unborn, and who will pass laws to prohibit abortions except to save the life of the mother. We need to vote for Senators and the President who will do the same, appointing and confirming Pro-Life judges to the Supreme Court. We need to support Crisis Pregnancy Centers and other organizations that support unwed mothers, as well as agencies that place babies for adoption. It is vital that the government and faith-based organizations assist in every way possible, pregnant women who don't want or can't afford to keep their babies. We must realize that every life is precious in the sight of God and act accordingly. It is long past time for our nation to return to the God of the Bible and to let His absolute truths again form the bedrock of our laws and behavior. Then we can stop the downward slide of immorality as we respect the right to life of every human being, both born and unborn.

Pat Moran was born and raised in Berea Ohio. He is a 1975 graduate of the US Air Force Academy. He flew for 12 years on active duty and then served for 17 years in the Reserves as an Academy Liaison Officer. He flew for Delta Air Lines for 30 years, retiring in 2018. He is a born again Christian and lives in Crittenden, Kentucky with his wife Cindy and has 7 grown children.

> *"Let everyone be subject to the governing authorities, for there is no authority except that which God has established. The authorities that exist have been established by God."*
> *Romans 13:1 (NIV)*

CHAPTER 22

RESPECT FOR AUTHORITY

BY PAUL MOCK

THE CLASSROOM SETTING in grade school and high school is as near important in childhood development as the family experience. When I was in school, respect for teachers and administrators was demanded and expected. Those who deviated were met with an internal district disciplinary process meant to influence attitudes and modify behavior. Those on the extremes were met with the harsher reality of the juvenile justice system. I remember being subject to the disciplinary process due to my own personal behaviors. The few times

I received discipline, I admitted my actions were wrong but never considered that a disrespectful reaction to the authority figure was proper or warranted. I was once the subject of corporal punishment in the seventh grade. I became the target of a large, double-layered paddle with holes drilled in it. The only requirement I was aware of prior to receiving the "swat" was parental permission. On learning of my disruptive behavior my mother told the vice-principal, "You give him one for me." Respect for authority and proper behavior was demanded from the home front.

I contrast my school experiences with what is contemporary respect for teachers and administrators today. I was informed of a recent experience of a grade schoolteacher who was surprised at the disrespectful attitude of many of the students. The teacher's observation was a direct correlation to what the students experienced in the home. Many students were in single-parent families (broken homes) – many without the father figure in the picture.[1] In one parent/teacher conference the mother of the child had offensive tattoos prominently displayed on her body. Not to minimize any serious home issues that the young student was experiencing, the example of lack of respect for authority that the parent modeled was evident. Sadly, many school administrators are adhering to

1-https://www.ncjrs.gov/pdffiles1/ojjdp/frd030127.pdf

a mantra of making everyone successful, don't offend anyone, and anything goes; much of which leads to a culture of mediocrity in the public-school systems as well as the students' lack of respect for authority. One only read California's SB 419 which make suspensions of students far more difficult.[2] Where California goes, so goes the rest of the Nation?

The recent rash of mass shootings and murders in our cities across the Nation is symptomatic of a shift in values and cultural mores. Something has seriously changed in our Nation's society since I was a kid. There is just something wrong with those who commit such atrocious acts of violence; acts that were unthinkable in the 1950s and 1960s. So, what has changed in our communities and society that has created such disrespect by so many towards authority and society? Young people do things differently today than they did just two generations past.

There is not just one reason. I believe it is a culmination of many influences and trends that have modeled a desensitizing of a portion of our society of values and mores that many have held as sacrosanct. A frightening number of the younger generation have developed anti-social behaviors which include: lack of respect for

2-https://leginfo.legislature.ca.gov/faces/billNavClient.xhtml?bill_id=201920200SB419

others, self-esteem issues, lack of confidence in themselves, shortfalls in verbal and non-verbal communications and fantasy thinking. There is a multitude of addictive video games where the "more you kill the better you score." Those with few outside interests and difficulty interacting with peers find themselves immersed in an electronic world where anything goes and "the game" becomes reality and becomes their center of focus for prolonged periods of time.[3] The addition of the smartphone enables the extension of the fantasy world to any corner. Pornography in its most graphic forms is a click away and easily available for anyone who desires to access it. Some music genres render the female sex as no more than sex objects deserving of no respect or value. Across the Nation there have been many instances of the removal of historical National artifacts that some have viewed offensive. Legalized late-term abortion has much support across the Nation. Suicide rates and assisted suicide is more common. Human life, respect for authority, heritage and others is devalued.

Much of my twenty-five years with the Los Angeles Police Department was in uniform. I worked several years in lower income, minority neighborhoods. I served with a great number

3-http://www.center4research.org/violent-video-games-can-increase-aggression/

of outstanding officers who were as honest and trustworthy as the code of conduct demanded. Respect for authority and others is expected within the ranks. Police academies across the Nation train a similar Law Enforcement Code of Ethics as established in 1957 by the IACP:

> As a law enforcement officer, my
> fundamental duty is to serve the
> community; to safeguard lives and
> property; to protect the innocent
> against deception, the weak against
> oppression or intimidation and the
> peaceful against violence or disorder;
> and to respect the constitutional rights
> of all to liberty, equality, and justice.[4]

Those who violate the code are subject to a disciplinary process. Most officers serve to this standard as it is intrinsic to their nature, not an imposed requirement. Today, the lack of respect for the authority of the law enforcement officer is shameful. It is fueled in part by those in positions of influence and power who desire to see progressive and socialist ideologies the norm. Preference to 'special groups' who advocate anarchy and 'liberties' over the law-abiding tax paying citizens' right to live productive, secure and safe lives is prevalent.

Way back, in the 1970s, a common observation

4-. https://www.theiacp.org/resources/law-enforcement-code-of-ethics

was the number of juvenile offenders who were raised in fatherless homes.[5] Many were raised by grandparents or others who would attempt to provide and care for them. Unfortunately, many of these grandparents are no longer available. The kids who were raised by grandparents are now the grandparents. The cycle continues and much remains true today. Broken homes is a just an occasional topic of discussion within the media and sadly, no actions have solved it. Children reared in a two-parent household seem to stand a better chance at developing a firmer footing with life, relationships and career. There are always exceptions, but the two-parent nuclear family provides a generally better grounding for kids growing up. Respect for authority and consistent modeling of values and character are more consistent. There is a relationship between kids brought up with a respect for authority, the law and social codes of conduct than those not. Arrest rates for kids raised with the disadvantage of broken homes are much higher as is their disrespect for authority, laws and the Golden Rule, "Do unto others as you would have them do unto you."

Disturbingly, some politicians at the national, state and local levels have voiced their support for non-cooperation of local law enforcement with

5-http://fathers.com/statistics-and-research/the-extent-of-fatherlessness/

American Military Veterans

ICE (*Immigration and Customs Enforcement*) to the open advocacy to abolish ICE. The false narrative of excessive police use of deadly force on minorities is proclaimed in the media by activists and politicians alike.[6] Such anti-law enforcement sentiments coupled with politically sanctioned sanctuary cities fuel distrust of law enforcement and the rule of law. Law enforcement officers take an oath: *to **respect** the constitutional rights of all to liberty, equality, and justice.* Unfortunately, in too many stances it is not reciprocal.

Anyone who has served in the military understands respect for authority. Respect is always earned and is two-way between those supervising/leading others and those being supervised/led. Legal orders are to be understood and followed. Many times, Soldiers' lives and the lives of others depend on respect and trust of others up and down the chain of command. Members of the military train repetitiously as individuals and units to ensure accomplishment of the mission. Inarguably, our military is comprised of the finest America has to offer. These men and women are the Nation's treasure and man the greatest fighting force the world has ever known. Disciplinary actions are rare but usually swift and fair as the great majority of military members intrinsically want to

---

6-https://www.manhattan-institute.org/html/deadly-shootings-ignored

serve to the best of their ability. Members of the Army are instilled with the Army Core Values;

> *"Loyalty, Duty, Respect, Selfless Service, Honor, Integrity and Personal Courage." Respect is defined in the Army Core Value as: Treat people as they should be treated. This is the same as do unto others as you would have done to you. (Army Regulation 600-100)*

After military service, most Veterans become valued, productive members of society who respect the opportunities the Nation has to offer. While serving as National Chair, Employer Support of the Guard and Reserve (ESGR), I experienced first-hand the support for those with military experience. Government leaders at all levels, CEOs of major corporations and small business owners attest their support for our Veterans and members of the National Guard and Reserve. I personally asked several business and community leaders why they like this group as potential employees? Repeatedly the response was; they are on-time, team players, drug free, accept constructive criticism, loyal and respectful. They have values and are a sought-after cohort among the Nation's employers.

There are many positive programs available. Junior ROTC, ROTC, military service, sports programs, faith-based service and missions, internships, trade schools to develop career skills to name a few. As an example of a great program that develops character and virtue among our young men and women are the Scouts BSA (formerly, Boy Scouts of America). Boys and girls from all races, religions and creeds enter the scouting program in grade school and are taught The Scout Law:

A Scout is:

TRUSTWORTHY. *Tell the truth and keep promises. People can depend on you.*

LOYAL. *Show that you care about your family, friends, Scout leaders, school, and country.*

HELPFUL. *Volunteer to help others without expecting a reward.*

FRIENDLY. *Be a friend to everyone, even people who are very different from you.*

COURTEOUS. *Be polite to everyone and always use good manners.*

KIND. *Treat others as you want to be*

*treated . Never harm or kill any living
thing without good reason.*

OBEDIENT. *Follow the rules of your
family, school, and pack. Obey the laws
of your community and country.*

CHEERFUL. *Look for the bright side
of life. Cheerfully do tasks that come
your way. Try to help others be happy.*

THRIFTY. *Work to pay your own way.
Try not to be wasteful. Use time, food,
supplies, and natural resources wisely.*

BRAVE. *Face difficult situations even
when you feel afraid. Do what you think
is right despite what others might be
doing or saying.*

CLEAN. *Keep your body and mind fit.
Help keep your home and community
clean.*

REVERENT. *Be reverent toward God.
Be faithful in your religious duties.
Respect the beliefs of others.*

Young men and women are taught that the
Scout Law is a model for their future development
as adolescents and adults, supported by caring
parents and adult-leaders will be provided every
opportunity for success in life. What more could

we ask? Programs such as Scouting teach respect for others and are a gateway for life success, if only afforded the opportunity.

We now live in a politically divided society. There will never be, nor should there be, one train of thought, right or left. There must be some level of balance. About respect, if we as citizens, families and leaders fail to respond, forces and time will forever change the face of our great Nation. We have already seen the impacts on our Nation and Communities as a result of our changing attitudes and behaviors as we lose respect for authority, others and our Nation's heritage. Carnage in our cities, murder of police officers, mass shootings, disrespect of teachers and leaders, disrespect for authority and others are symptomatic of a society in trouble.

Those in positions of influence (business, faith based, community, government, media, sports and elected leaders) *must* first admit there is a problem that must be fixed and put this critical social crisis as a priority. Respect for life, authority, neighbors, family, peers, educators must be voiced publicly, modeled and lived daily. Personal responsibility and accountability must be demanded at all levels. Only when the scales tip towards a more respectful society will society's equilibrium be restored.

According to statistics reported to the FBI, 106 law enforcement officers were killed in line-of-duty incidents in 2018. Of these, 55 officers died as a result of felonious acts, and 51 officers died in accidents.

The number of officers killed as a result of criminal acts in 2018 was 9 more than the 46 officers who were feloniously killed in 2017. The 5- and 10-year comparisons show an increase of 4 felonious deaths compared with the 2014 and an increase of 7 deaths compared with 2009.[1]

1-https://www.fbi.gov/news/pressrel/press-releases/fbi-releases-2018-statistics-on-law-enforcement-officers-killed-in-the-line-of-duty

Major General (Retired) Paul Mock served twenty-five years with the Los Angeles Police Department. He was commissioned in 1972 through ROTC and served thirty-six years in the Guard and Reserve. After retirement, he served four years as the National Chair, Employer Support of the Guard and Reserves (ESGR). He was born in California and now resides in Texas.

SIT-REP

It was during the battle for the Chosin Reservoir, at an airstrip in Koto-ri, that the commanding officer of the 7th Marines, Lewis (Chesty) Puller was reputed to have summed up the situation like this:

> *"They're on our right; they're on our left; they're in front of us; they're behind us. They can't get away now!"*

CHAPTER 23

THE SIT-REP
FINAL WORDS

BY SKIP CORYELL

THIS FINAL CHAPTER CAN be viewed as a military situation report on the status of America, and it's not looking good.

America is predominantly a two-party political system, and one-half of that system has become a staunch advocate for socialism in America. I grew up in the sixties, during a time when communism was seen as the number one threat to freedom world-wide. It was the height of the Cold War, America was embroiled in Vietnam, and, unknown to me, my friend and mentor, Denny

Gillem, was fighting in the jungle to stop the communist advance throughout IndoChina.

I remember quite vividly, as a 12-year-old boy, reading the book *Alas Babylon*, by Pat Frank. The novel is set in the aftermath of an all-out nuclear war, as one small community in Florida struggles to survive. That novel had a profound effect on me.

The year was 1969, and I remember many nights I would stand outside in my front yard on a summer night, staring to the north at the lights in the sky a scant 30 miles away at the city of Grand Rapids, and I couldn't help but wonder ... is tonight the night? Will I wake up tomorrow, or will I be incinerated in my bed while I sleep by a Soviet missile?

I was a child of the H-bomb, growing up in the shadow of nuclear annihilation, believing that, even if I survived the Cold War, I would soon be old enough to fight and die in the rice paddy of a far-off land. It was a pretty bleak sit-rep for a 12-year-old boy.

But here's the rub ... I survived. America survived. All of us still live and breathe and flourish in a land defined by freedom at every turn. The Soviet Union fell, and was replaced with a lesser tyrant, but still a tyrant and still a threat.

Later, when I joined the Marine Corps, I swore an oath to protect and defend the Constitution of the United States against all enemies, both foreign and domestic. Today, at 62 years of age, I look at America, not through the eyes of a young, naive boy, untested and untried, but as a military veteran, one who has volunteered and trained in order to protect and defend our great nation.

America is special, but this has always been the case. Any patriot, any serious student of history, knows this to be true.

> *But still ... we stand teetered on the brink of socialism.*

And let's be honest here: socialism is nothing more than *Communism Lite*. If you liken it to a beer, then it has half the calories, but all the tyranny.

President Reagan nailed it when he said:

> *"Freedom is never more than one generation away from extinction. We didn't pass it to our children in the bloodstream. It must be fought for, protected, and handed on for them to do the same."*

The plan of attack on America was laid out by Nikita Khrushchev way back in 1959.

> *"We cannot expect the Americans to jump from capitalism to communism, but we can assist their elected leaders in giving Americans small doses of*

socialism, until they suddenly awake to find they have communism."

Socialism is the gateway drug to communism.

So what is the situation report today? Is Khrushchev's prediction coming true?

I think the answer to that question is entirely up to us, because the future hasn't been written yet. I believe American freedom is on the ropes. I believe that if any of the Founding Fathers were to wake up and see America right now, they would immediately take up arms and mobilize the militia.

But here's one big distinction between 1776 and today: we still have enough of our freedoms left with which to fight and defend the Constitution. And our number one freedom is ensconced in what we say and do and write.

Here are some things you can do as a patriotic American that will help us win this war to save America.

1. Get informed.

The Founders cautioned us against ignorance and complacency.

Knowledge will forever govern ignorance: And a people who mean to be their own Governors, must arm themselves with the power which knowledge gives.

— James Madison

While I understand that many conservatives and independents don't want to be heavily involved in politics, I also understand that the far-left is the usurper of all things left unattended.

Politics tends to draw the greedy among us and those who wish to accumulate power. Because of this, it's paramount that we educate ourselves and not just vote, but also to run for office. If you can't run, then support those good people who do.

But heed this: if you choose to remain ignorant, then you will likely someday be ruthlessly ruled by another of lesser virtue. History is rife with lessons that teach: "there is always one segment of society who wants to rule his fellow man."

2. Get rebellious.

Freedom has never been for the faint of heart. Have you ever wondered why there are so few countries willing to stand up and fight to establish their own freedom? Most nations simply bask in the warm glow of America's liberty. I used to wonder why other countries didn't stand up to tyrants and seize liberty. Perhaps they lack the courage? Perhaps they've been "ruled" for so long that they have no concept or picture of freedom in their hearts and minds?

Conservatives tend to be very polite; they just

want to work hard, provide for their family, mind their own business and then fade away into obscurity. But here's the problem with that: sheep cannot stay free. The wolf will always come and do as he wishes to those who passively accept his vicious will.

Again, our Founders had something to say about standing up to fight for freedom.

> *"Is life so dear, or peace so sweet, as to be purchased at the price of chains and slavery? Forbid it, Almighty God! I know not what course others may take, but as for me, give me liberty or give me death!"*
>
> *—Patrick Henry*

> *"Our unalterable resolution should be to be free."*
>
> *—Samuel Adams*

> *"The sacred rights of mankind are not to be rummaged for among old parchments or musty records. They are written, as with a sunbeam, in the whole volume of human nature, by the hand of the divinity itself, and can never be erased or obscured by mortal power."*
>
> *—Alexander Hamilton*

American Military Veterans

Freedom is worth fighting for. So battle hard and battle long. Stand up to anyone who would make you subservient. Most political battles can be fought with a simple lever in a voting machine, but we must also speak out boldly against those who would subjugate us and our progeny.

3. Educate the young.

> *"Train up a child in the way he should go: and when he is old, he will not depart from it."*
>
> *Proverbs 22:6 (KJV)*

I'm guessing that most reading this book are not in college. You are probably much older. But that means that you have children and grandchildren who are within your sphere of influence. Public education can no longer be trusted to pass on freedom's torch, so you must do it for the children you love. Speak to the young folks in your life every chance you get. Chances are they've been fed socialist doctrine their entire lives, and you may be the only voice of reason they ever hear.

Parents, raise your kids grounded in basic civics. Make them read the *Constitution* and the *Declaration of Independence* as well as the other writings of our Founding Fathers. And then sit down and discuss it with them.

Frontlines of Freedom

My wife is an Aerospace Engineer by trade. She sacrificed her career and a six-figure salary to stay home and educate our three children. But is that really such a great sacrifice compared to what our Founders gave to all of us in order to procure through bloodshed, our original freedom? I think not.

> *"And for the support of this Declaration, with a firm reliance on the protection of Divine Providence, we mutually pledge to each other our Lives, our Fortunes, and our sacred Honor."*
>
> —*Closing statement*
> *Declaration of Independence*

Many signers of the *Declaration of Independence*, indeed paid the price for the liberty we now enjoy. Please ... pass on freedom's torch to the next generation.

4. Become moral.

This may very well be the hardest sell of all, and that's why I save it for last. It also is the toughest to enact. Immorality is an easy sell. It's easy to be greedy, to be selfish, to always act in your own best interest, regardless of what harm it does to others. Greed has an instant pay-off. Selfishness gives us immediate gratification. Sloth, taking something for nothing, is a siren, calling out from deep inside the bowels of socialism that reaches into the basest and darkest parts of the human soul. Resist the sirens. Cover your ears. They lead to a predictable and inevitable destination.

Chains and slavery.

It is easy to cheat on your spouse. All you have to do is relax and give in to your carnal, animal desires.

But it is difficult to rebuff the advances of a beautiful, and younger woman who can feed your ego and physical appetites.

Giving in to selfishness is easy, has an immediate pay-off and is difficult to resist.

It is easy to cheat your employer by leaving early. But the act damages your soul and erodes away at your natural sense of right and wrong as well as your self-respect.

Resist immorality in all its forms. Instead, embrace virtue.

> *"The only foundation of a free*
> *Constitution, is pure Virtue, and if this*
> *cannot be inspired into our People, in*
> *a great Measure, than they have it now.*
> *They may change their Rulers, and the*
> *forms of Government, but they will not*
> *obtain a lasting Liberty."*
>
> *–John Adams*

Frontlines of Freedom

There can be no free nation absent moral virtue. Immorality is selfishness run amok, and serves as food for tyrants.

Whatever your religion, please take some time to think about it. There is no place for greed and selfishness in a lasting republic.

Okay, it seems I'm running out of pages, and I'm in dire danger of preaching. So let me get to the heart of the matter.

Here's the sit-rep.

> *If the present course of human events is not altered; if we do not return to the beliefs and teachings of the Founding Fathers, then America cannot endure as a free country.*

I remember vividly growing up in the sixties. There was this wonderful saying that the hippies loved, and, that later on, many respectable Americans bought into. It went like this:

> *"If it feels good ...do it."*

The destination of that world-in-life view is a foregone conclusion. It has taken us to where we are today. If you don't like where America is headed, then it is incumbent upon you to change it. No one else can do it ... only you. That must be your attitude.

Let me close with one final recommendation. Here's a formula for happiness and freedom that has always worked, no matter when or where it was tried:

> *"If my people, which are called by my name, shall humble themselves, and pray, and seek my face, and turn from their wicked ways; then will I hear from heaven, and will forgive their sin, and will heal their land."*
>
> *2 Chronicles 7:14 (KJV)*

We have the high ground, and a man who never gives up cannot be beaten. The battle is ours to lose.

> *"They're on our right; they're on our left; they're in front of us; they're behind us. They can't get away now!"*

On behalf of the authors of this book, we thank you for reading *Frontlines of Freedom* and considering our views.

And now ... go forth and conquer.

"But the real hero is the man who fights even though he's scared. Some men will get over their fright in a minute under fire, some take an hour, and for some it takes days. But the real man never lets his fear of death overpower his honor, his sense of duty to his country, and his innate manhood."

—George S. Patton

Skip Coryell lives with his wife and children in Michigan. He is the author of *Concealed Carry for Christians* and *Civilian Combat: The Concealed Carry Book*. He is an avid hunter and sportsman, a Marine Corps veteran, and a graduate of Cornerstone University. You can listen to Skip as he co-hosts the syndicated military talk radio show *Frontlines of Freedom* on frontlinesoffreedom.com. You can also hear his weekly podcast *The Home Defense Show* at homedefenseshow.com.

For more details on Skip Coryell, or to contact him personally, go to his website at skipcoryell.com.

The Bill of Rights

1–Congress shall make no law respecting an establishment of religion, or prohibiting the free exercise thereof; or abridging the freedom of speech, or of the press; or the right of the people peaceably to assemble, and to petition the Government for a redress of grievances.

2– A well regulated Militia, being necessary to the security of a free State, the right of the people to keep and bear Arms, shall not be infringed.

3– No Soldier shall, in time of peace be quartered in any house, without the consent of the Owner, nor in time of war, but in a manner to be prescribed by law.

4– The right of the people to be secure in their persons, houses, papers, and effects, against unreasonable searches and seizures, shall not be violated, and no Warrants shall issue, but upon probable cause, supported by Oath or affirmation, and particularly describing the place to be searched, and the persons or things to be seized.

5– No person shall be held to answer for a capital, or otherwise infamous crime, unless on a presentment or indictment of a Grand Jury, except in cases arising in the land or naval forces, or in the Militia, when in actual service in time of War or public danger; nor shall any person be subject for the same offence to be twice put in jeopardy of life or limb; nor shall be compelled in any criminal case to be a witness against himself, nor be deprived of life, liberty, or property, without due process of law; nor shall private property be taken for public use, without just compensation.

6– In all criminal prosecutions, the accused shall enjoy the right to a speedy and public trial, by an impartial jury of the State and district wherein the crime shall have been committed, which district shall have been previously ascertained by law, and to be informed of the nature and cause of the accusation; to be confronted with the witnesses against him; to have compulsory process for obtaining witnesses in his favor, and to have the Assistance of Counsel for his defense.

7– In suits at common law, where the value in controversy shall exceed twenty dollars, the right of trial by jury shall be preserved, and no fact tried by a jury, shall be otherwise re-examined in any court of the United States, than according to the rules of the common law.

8– Excessive bail shall not be required, nor excessive fines imposed, nor cruel and unusual punishments inflicted.

9– The enumeration in the Constitution, of certain rights, shall not be construed to deny or disparage others retained by the people.

10– The powers not delegated to the United States by the Constitution, nor prohibited by it to the States, are reserved to the States respectively, or to the people.

FRONTLINES OF FREEDOM RADIO

You can hear authors Denny Gillem and
Skip Coryell on one of your local stations
on the number 1 military talk show in America. *Frontlines of Freedom* is syndicated on
over 180 stations, and is also available as a
podcast on frontlinesoffreedom.com.

Publisher's Note

The many beautiful photographs in this book were taken by friend and patriot, Rick Vuyst. Rick is the author of the book *Operation Rumination*.

In his book, Rick delves into his own personal thoughts as one of the 92.7 percent who never served in the military. To understand better he spent a year with veterans listening to their stories. In the process he wrestled with the fact he never served and reflects on the freedoms he enjoys because of the service and sacrifice of others. Rick's books as well as his beautiful photography can be found at www.thankyouverymulch.com.

Frontlines of Freedom